Real Parenting

Using Real Colors® to Better Understand Your Child

Written by Dr. Dan Johnson

for

National Curriculum & Training Institute,® Inc.

For further information on **Real Colors**® or NCTI please contact:

National Curriculum & Training Institute®, Inc.
P.O. Box 60905 • Phoenix, AZ 85082-0905

(800) 622-1644 • E-Mail: info@ncti.org

Or visit our Web site at www.realcolors.org

Printed in China.

ISBN 0-9754153-3-6

Contents

Introduction

This guide is the third in a series of manuals designed to help you apply **Real Colors**® concepts to your daily life. Having attended a **Real Colors** workshop, you have been introduced to the power of temperament in helping you understand yourself and others. Although it is not absolutely necessary, you will find it helpful to have read *The Real Colors Homeowner's Guide* and *The Real Colors Relationships Guide*. The *"Homeowner's Guide"* provides useful tips on developing a deeper understanding of your own personality: where your Blue, Gold, Green, and Orange characteristics come from, what they look like in action, and how you can balance the reality of who you are within the context of your everyday life. The *"Relationships Guide"* extends this understanding to your relationships with friends, family, and other individuals.

Real Parenting moves beyond the scope of self. In home building you are designing your own life with some recognition of how you can get along better with others. In relationship building you are balancing your needs with other people's needs in order to enrich your life. In parenting, however, you must recognize that you are dealing with something beyond yourself. Although the rewards of parenthood are many, if you go into parenting with an expectation of being rewarded and enriched on a daily basis, you may be in for a big surprise.

Introduction

Keeping with the **Real Colors**® philosophy that people need concrete examples to bring personality concepts to life, I have chosen an architectural analogy for this parenting guide. Some might have suggested an artist analogy such as a sculptor. But sculptors create masterpieces that express their dreams and inner thoughts. Architects design possibilities for the person who will make a house their home. Then they hand off the design concept to engineers and contractors who may provide further modifications to meet the homeowner's needs and aspirations.

Parenting is more of an art than a science. Parenting is dynamic, its demands shifting with a child's innate nature and life experiences. Opening yourself to parenting responsibilities carries with it both opportunities and obstacles. It takes a willingness to risk, to trust yourself, your partner, your family, teachers, and other adult caregivers. But most importantly, it requires you to trust your child, to design a home environment (a model of decision making) that allows your child ultimate flexibility to become who he or she wants to become.

As an architect you need to think about the following guidelines:

1. *Know what quality architecture (building a **Real Colors** home) looks like.*

2. *Ask the homeowner questions and listen to the answers.*

3. *Know the building codes in your community.*

Introduction

4. *Focus on the homeowner's fundamental values and apply your skills to enhance them.*

5. *Manipulate your drawings rather than manipulating the homeowner.*

In the first chapter of this manual you will review the characteristics of each Color. This chapter reminds you how to use the Colors as an architectural touchstone to provide life experiences for children so that they can build the home that suits their needs rather than your needs.

In chapter two you will learn how to ask questions of, observe, and listen to children. The purpose of this chapter is to learn to look closely at the clues that indicate your child's primary and follow-up Colors. As an architect you need to think carefully about how your Color preferences can either promote or impede your child's personal growth.

In chapter three you will be encouraged to consider the community in which your child's home is being constructed. It is not easy to build a three story modern home within a community of ranch homes. It's fine to be your Color, but you had better learn to do all of the Colors.

Chapter four focuses on the homeowner's fundamental values. Parents need to help children build on their natural Color preferences. A good Color balance is derived from enhancing strengths rather than overcoming liabilities. Remember, a liability is simply a strength that we carry too far.

Introduction

In chapter five you will be reminded once again that the home you are designing belongs to the homeowner, not to you. Parents need to focus on planning for and responding to childhood experiences rather than manipulating their children. Good architects offer options to a homeowner. They help the homeowner see a potential home from numerous perspectives before choosing the final architectural design.

In chapter six you will explore how to help your child develop a balance between being his or her primary Color and learning to do and appreciate other Colors. As with relationships, there are no magic bullets for effective parenting. But there are numerous lenses through which you can differentiate between what you want for your child based on your past experiences and what your child needs and prefers to be happy in his or her future. **Real Colors**® provides a touchstone for such considerations. Good luck with improving your parenting skills. Influencing a child's life in positive ways is one of the most challenging and enriching experiences of your life. As you work at it, be certain to appreciate and enjoy your work. The pleasure you take from this experience will have a significant impact on the pleasure your child will take from it.

UNDERSTANDING REAL COLORS® ARCHITECTURE

1

PLAN
ECH.: 1/8"

Understanding Real Colors® Architecture

Parenting is both an awesome joy and an awesome responsibility. In fact, most other human responsibilities pale next to the responsibilities involved with parenthood. All parents want to handle their responsibilities effectively. But what does effective parenting look like? This *Real Colors® Parenting Guide* is designed to help you explore this question.

The National Curriculum and Training Institute, creators of **Real Colors®**, believes that effectiveness is a shifting target defined by people's perceptions. Perceptions, in turn, result from a combination of the person we want to be and the person we need to be.

In *The Real Colors Homeowner's Guide* (2004) we emphasized the role that the Colors can play in an individual life. We referred to the **Real Colors** System as a home for your personality. When you become comfortable in applying the Colors to your life, you feel safe enough to invite others into your world and, in turn, you can feel more relaxed in their world.

In *The Real Colors Relationship Guide* (2006) our analogy shifted from the house itself to the table inside that house. We focused on sharing that table (who we are) with another person — so that we could establish a meaningful relationship with a friend or significant other. We focused on the concept that forming such relationships makes each party stronger and at the same time more vulnerable. What then happens when you throw off all the garbs of your personal Color preferences in order to help your children appreciate and develop their Color preferences?

Understanding Real Colors® Architecture

Welcome to the world of **Real Colors**® parenting. This is a world in which it helps to have a strong sense of who you are as an individual and who you and your spouse are as a couple. Even in a divorced or blended family situation, the relationship shared by parents must be clear and consistent in order to help children develop a realistic appreciation of their Color preferences.

In the parent-child relationship, you (the adult) are helping your children design a house that they will inhabit to some degree or another for the rest of their lives. It's their house, not your house. In parenting you are the architect. You bring a vast array of skills to the architectural table because of the significant amount of life experiences you have had. But if your drawings don't feel good to your children, or if they don't create a house that meets their needs, protects them from unwanted elements, or allows them to entertain friends as they desire, they will not use your plans to construct their home. They may comply with the plans as long as they are required to do so, or they may follow them with a little resistance until something better comes along.

When Luis and Janet were expecting their first child, Carlos, they spent hours talking about their dreams and aspirations as parents. Janet is an Orange-Blue salesperson who has never met a stranger. She is outgoing, witty, and one of the top salespersons in her pharmaceutical company.

Janet's clients actually look forward to her calls. They tell her that her humorous stories and her ability to bring a smile to their day is the best medicine she carries – and they come free.

Luis is a Green-Gold attorney who moved to a part-time position so that he could continue his career but have more time to be with the baby. Unlike Janet, Luis is serious and highly organized – witty but not necessarily funny or outgoing. Luis' friends were not surprised when he decided to be a part-time stay-at-home dad. It made logical sense that he would lay aside any concerns about male stereotypes regarding parenting. After all, Luis' law practice allowed more flexibility than Janet's position in sales.

Luis and Janet often laugh about how "non-traditional" their relationship is. *"I'm the stereotype of the male role,"* Janet laughs. *"I'm always looking for the next adventure, never on time for dinner, and always anxious to buy typical "boy toys."*

"And I keep the home fires burning and the family organized – like a good house-husband," adds Luis.

But Luis and Janet want what most parents want for their children. They want Carlos to be happy, well adjusted, and successful. They want him to be confident without being arrogant. They want him to have friends without losing sight of his own sense of self.

> The first step in getting along with others is getting along with yourself – understanding and accepting who you are.

They want Carlos to have many positive life experiences, but they want to protect him from the pain and suffering that sometimes come with those experiences.

It is difficult, if not impossible, to change your Color order. And it is generally counterproductive to focus on your liabilities. A negative approach generally will not get you the balance you are seeking (or that others would prefer). It may even decrease your ability to excel in your preferred Color.

Understanding Real Colors® Architecture

Janet and Luis want to be effective parents. They understand their own Color preferences and appreciate what each brings to their relationship table. Janet wonders how their "non-traditional" relationship will affect their child's development. What will happen when Luis takes Carlos to a birthday party or to pre-school? Will Carlos wonder why his mommy isn't there with all the other mommies? Will Luis be able to join in with the moms for carpooling and other activities? Will Luis be left out of the loop, and will that mean that Carlos may be left out of the loop as well?

Luis simply suggests that he will be very popular with the moms because he can spare them the hassle of taking their sons into the ladies restroom. *"And just think how popular I will be when I can remove the mayonnaise lid or lift the boys onto my shoulders at the park,"* he adds.

Janet and Luis have a good sense of their **Real Colors**® strengths. The fundamental message of the **Real Colors** system is that the first step in getting along with others is getting along with yourself – understanding and accepting who you are. Victor Frankl (1959) described this balance as a "search for meaning." Such meaning comes from being yourself and capitalizing on your strengths.

The balance between independence and getting along with others is seldom perfect and never static. The people and events of your world affect the range and intensity of your Colors and the range and intensity of your relationships. Parenting is not about correcting what your parents did wrong in raising you. It is about finding the balance between your aspirations for your children and their aspirations for themselves. If you listen to, observe, and support your children in good times and bad and encourage them to build on their strengths, they will learn to be their primary Color as they do the other three Colors more effectively. But in order to help your child accomplish this balance, you must have a firm understanding of your present and your past. How have you designed your own home? Or did you, in fact, design it? How much of the stuff in your Color home did you collect on your own, and how much was given to you by parents, teachers, colleagues, and friends?

In many ways parenting is an impossible undertaking. But while there are no guarantees for raising the perfect human being, an understanding of **Real Colors**® is a useful tool for thinking about your parental responsibilities.

Let's take a moment to review the aspects of the relationship table and the house in which this table has been placed. The following paragraphs are meant to be a summary of key Real Colors concepts. For a more in-depth review you may want to return to the *Homeowner's Guide* or the *Relationships Guide*.

A Homeowner's Review

In the Homeowner's Guide you were asked to think of your personality in terms of a four-room house. Each room of your house represents an aspect of your personality: who you are, how you take in and act upon the experiences of your everyday life. Do you tend to focus more on Blue issues of human relationships and the purpose of your existence within the overall flow of life? Do you focus on Gold issues of managing the day-to-day aspects of your life within a defined set of parameters? Do you focus on Green issues of logical consistency within a set of generally accepted scientific principles? Or do you focus on Orange issues of action where you place a priority on experiencing as much of life as possible within the time available to you?

The Basic Real Colors® Floor Plan
Figure 1.1

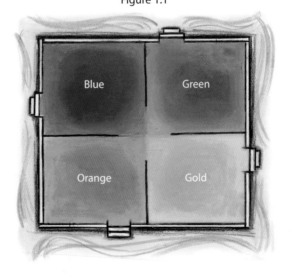

Understanding Real Colors® Architecture

Remember, each room in this house has its own exterior entrance. But as you know, you will tend to use one of these four entrances more than the other three, and once inside the house, you will spend more time in some rooms than in others. You can learn to use different entrances from time to time and to feel comfortable in any room, but when you become so accustomed to entering your house through the same door and spending most of your time in one or two rooms, you limit your ability to use the other rooms effectively. As you have learned, "A liability is the result of carrying a strength too far."

You may develop a strength to such an extent that you impede other aspects of your personality. You get so busy functioning in your preferred Color that you forget to develop other Colors. But what happens when parents, family, friends, and work responsibilities prevent you from spending enough time in your preferred room or from moving from room to room in the order that feels most comfortable to you? At these times you feel unappreciated.

Keirsey's research (1998) places Color percentages among the general population as shown at right.

(See www.keirsey.com for more current research statistics.)

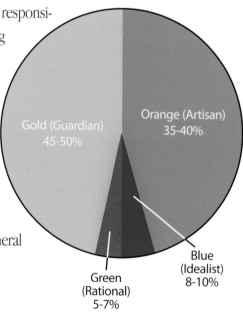

Gold (Guardian) 45-50%

Orange (Artisan) 35-40%

Blue (Idealist) 8-10%

Green (Rational) 5-7%

Understanding Real Colors® Architecture

Golds and Oranges find meaning in concrete, real world experiences. They focus on the real world through their senses of sight, hearing, smell, touch, and taste. Oranges are artisans who value facts and events as potential opportunities to discover and enjoy their world. Golds tend to be tactical, valuing facts and events that fit predefined parameters.

Blues and Greens search for meaning in a more abstract world — in connections that lie beyond facts and events. They function more intuitively focusing on the connections between and among people and events. Blues focus on the spiritual or emotional impact of facts and events. Greens focus on logical connections and underlying principles. Among these intuitive, big-picture folks, Blues outnumber Greens.

While both Golds and Oranges focus initially on concrete events and experiences, they process those experiences in different ways. Likewise, Blues and Greens both focus on connections among events and experiences, but they process those connections from significantly different perspectives. However, a more significant factor lies in the imbalance between concretes and abstracts. Oranges and Golds combined outnumber Blues and Greens combined by more than three to one. It is obviously easier for Golds or Oranges to find people who share their views. Since there are fewer Blues and Greens in the world, these abstract individuals find themselves having to fit in. On the other hand, their unique way of looking at the world can create a special demand for their abilities and services. The table below illustrates the significance of this imbalance.

The Concrete-Abstract Imbalance
Figure 1.15

CONCRETE
80-90%
of the population

ABSTRACT
13-17%
of the population

Gold
45-50%
Logistical

Orange
35-40%
Tactician

Blue
8-10%
Diplomat

Green
5-7%
Strategist

Let's shift our attention from how these individual characteristics interact with one another to how they form a balance within a relationship. Let's consider your place at the Relationship table.

Setting the Relationship Table

The parent-child relationship differs from other relationships in that only one of the parties has chosen to participate. As you look at Figure 1.2, taken from the Relationships Guide, ask yourself in which room you would set the table if your child were your primary guest – in your preferred room or in your child's preferred room.

Placing Your Relationship Table
Figure 1.2

Let's assume that as a Blue you have chosen to place your table in the Blue room, a bright room filled with art and soft music with flowers and artifacts from around the world. But how will the Blue room feel to your child? In other words, what Color is your child?

Surroundings are important, and they impact each Color in slightly different ways. Blues want their surroundings to communicate, *"I'm glad you're here. Relax and get comfortable. Your comfort is my most important priority at this moment."*

Greens may either ignore their surroundings entirely or focus on unique or even obscure qualities. *"I want to get to know you – what you think, how you think, why you think the way you do."*

Understanding Real Colors® Architecture

Golds appreciate orderly, secure surroundings. *"I need to have things in order so that I can focus on who you are and what we might have in common."*

Oranges generally appreciate informality. *"Let's not worry about the limp vegetables or the roast being overdone. Let's talk about golf and our next tournament."*

Regardless of where you choose to place the table, that decision will influence the factors that will define your relationship. What do we teach our children if we always set the table in their preferred room? What are we teaching them if we always place the table in our preferred room?

As with any other relationship, parents should remember to celebrate differences. Don't set out to change yourself for your child. But don't assume that your child is just like you. The key to positive parenting is for both parent and child to be who they are and to be able to do things that please one another. The complexity relative to parenting, however, is that you (the parent) hold the power card – for better or worse.

As you approach your relationship with your child, you may want to ask yourself whether you have found a wondrous balance between your two personalities or simply exercised your authority over your child's choices. You also need to remember that people often find themselves attracted to other people who display a very different Color rainbow. These differences can be very positive in a parent-child relationship, but they can also set the stage for sending children mixed messages. *"I think what you do is funny here at home, but it embarrasses me when you behave that way in front of other people."* OR, *"I encourage you to be independent as long as you don't veer too far from the path I have designed for you."*

For example, a Blue-Orange parent may find comfort in a Gold-Green child's sense of purpose and direction. A Gold-Blue parent may admire an Orange-Green child's wry sense of humor and willingness to push the envelope. But what happens when the Gold-Green child's sense of purpose gets in the way of the family's day of entertainment? What happens when the Orange-Blue child's sense of humor becomes sarcasm directed at you?

It is important to remember that the primary responsibility for establishing the parent-child relationship rests with you, the adult. But the primary responsibility for determining what becomes of that relationship rests with your child.

Lamberto is an Orange-Blue father who finds himself losing touch with his fourteen-year-old son, Paul. But Lamberto's wife, Paula, complains that Lamberto is too lenient with Paul. Throughout elementary school Paul was a conscientious, well-behaved, high achiever. Then in middle school Paul got into sports and became enthralled with the opposite sex. At first Lamberto thought Paul's antics were simply a part of growing up. *"I was the same way when I was his age,"* Lamberto would tell Paula. *"He'll outgrow this. I did. I would have outgrown it a lot sooner if my dad had been more under-standing instead of being such a drill sergeant."*

But as Paul has moved through middle school, he has found it more rewarding to be the class clown than to be the star student. He was popular with the guys, and the girls seemed willing to buy lottery tickets for the chance to walk down the hall with the good looking, popular athlete. Why should he struggle to get the teacher's approval when he can gain his friends' approval so much more easily by being funny? He has promised his dad that he would buckle down next quarter. But it has become more and more difficult to do well on tests that he hasn't studied for.

Recently Paul stepped over the line. One night during Christmas break of Paul's eighth grade year, Lamberto was called to pick Paul up at the police station. Paul had told Lamberto that he was staying over night at his friend Totter's house. But Paul and Totter had sneaked out after midnight and gone to a keg party. The police had picked them up when a neighbor called in a complaint about loud music and "carrying on." About eight kids ranging in age from 12 to 15 were drinking alcohol and smoking marijuana. One had opened the doors and moved the stereo speakers to the patio. They had ransacked the house, and one boy had been taken to the hospital after having aspirated on his own vomit.

Of course Lamberto was embarrassed. He was also angry because each of the boys' families had to pay $500 for damages at the house where the party was held. But more importantly, Lamberto felt violated. Paul had broken faith with him. Paul had promised earlier that same day that he would do better in school and stay out of trouble. He had also assured Lamberto that Totter and he would be working on a science project for school, playing some video games, and watching some movies. Had this been a spur of the moment indiscretion, Lamberto might have felt differently. But Paul had deliberately played him.

Since that night, Lamberto has refused to trust Paul about anything. They haven't done much together, and when they are together, they argue over the most trivial things. Paula tells Lamberto that he and Paul seem to be in a tug of war to see who will determine the future course of Paul's life. And both seem to be losing.

Both Paula and Lamberto and Janet and Luis, mentioned earlier, want to be good parents. But what does good parenting (effective parenting) look like? To be an effective parent, you first need to remember that you are not building a house for yourself or inviting a guest to your table for a pleasant evening. When you have a series of difficult experiences with a guest, you may not continue to invite them back to your table. That option does not exist in the parent-child relationship.

Designing A Home With Your Child

The first thing you need to know if you are going to be a good architect of human houses is that you are not designing this house for yourself. It is going to belong to another person – your child. Therefore, you need to find out what your child wants and needs, what your child values.

At the same time, as an educator I have learned that there is a significant correlation between adult expectations and children's performance (Kroeze and Johnson, 1997). I have also learned that in many situations there is a significant mismatch between how adults want their children to act and the behaviors that they as adults model for them.

Most human beings want everything – at least we think we do. The truth is that we want the positive aspects of what we see, without what we see as the negative aspects that accompany the positives. We never really outgrow this human dilemma. But as Piaget (1952) taught us, with experience we learn to adapt to or accommodate those aspects of our experiences that do not comply with our preconceived notions of our world.

In the first couple of years of childhood, parents should find as many positive experiences as possible to engage in with their children. Learn to look for clues of your children's preferences and needs, their values. It is important for architects to know what their customers want, and it is important for the homeowners to gain confidence in their architects. Effective human architects don't simply observe what their children do. They ask questions to find out why they choose a particular action or response.

Very young children have difficulty expressing their ideas in terms that an adult can understand. But it would probably be safe to suggest that in at least 95% of cases this inability to express ideas comes from a lack of experience rather than a lack of ability. With very young children it is necessary and appropriate for parent-architects to observe and interpret the child-builder's values. As you provide experiences for your children, watch what makes them happy – how much they seek security and comfort versus how much they seek risk and adventure. Remember, children do not have a plethora of experiences to draw from. Their early years are a series of discoveries. Many of their daily experiences are risks. It is a risk to leave the comfort of mom's arms, frightening to be alone and unable to fend for

Understanding Real Colors® Architecture

yourself, frustrating to want something that you cannot articulate, and dangerous to take a first step when you have little sense of balance or depth perception.

It is important for human architects to recognize the blend of their abilities and the homeowner's values. Your child's Color home exists within the Color home that you and your spouse have built together. It is important to share your values with your children. It is equally important to explain the reasons underlying those values. Why do you do the things you do? Why do they work for you? What are the parameters within which your children must build their home? Do you have hot buttons? If so, who is responsible for avoiding them: you or your child?

Be certain to let your children know what the rules of the game are. And be certain to explain that as a parent you only control a small piece of the building codes in the community. Schools, churches, and communities have certain social norms that are much easier to navigate if you know how to recognize them. Building codes are not designed to impede your children's construction but to enhance and sustain it. The building codes give the architect and the builder a way to manage a complex project. Life is a balance of being yourself while valuing the right of other people to be themselves. Hidden agendas hurt both the architect and the builder. The child or homeowner knows what he wants at that particular moment but may not be aware of the consequences of these preferences. Architects bring their skills to the table and know what the expectations for construction are within the greater community. Building codes protect the architect and the homeowner.

Again, I like to think of the four Colors in terms of what I have called the Four-P's (Johnson, 2005). Figure 1.3 lists each of these P's by Color along with a question designed to guide your thinking as you apply the Color to real life situations.

The 4-P's

Figure 1.3

Color	Four-Ps	Four-P Questions
Blue	Purpose	What makes this important?
Gold	Parameters	What are the rules of the game?
Green	Principles	How will I make this work?
Orange	Priorities	Will it make a difference?

Every human being is born with the capability of functioning in each of the four Colors. In fact, it is impossible to function in life without addressing all of them. By thinking of the Colors in terms of the Four-P's, you can begin to see how you have shaped critical life decisions for yourself. Then you can learn to communicate and model these practices with your children.

Remember, people give you clues about their Colors through their words and actions. Effective architects learn to listen for clues as illustrated in Figure 1.4.

Listening for Color Clues
Figure 1.4

When a Blue is pleased...	When a Blue is agitated...
What would you like to do today?	Why can't people be more understanding about...?
When a Gold is pleased...	**When a Gold is agitated...**
Let's get our work finished or we can't...	Why can't people be more responsible when it comes to...?
When a Green is pleased...	**When a Green is agitated...**
I think we ought to look at this situation more closely...	If people only took the time to think about...
When an Orange is pleased...	**When an Orange is agitated...**
Hey, I know! Let's...	I wish someone would do something; anything would be better than...

As a parent you must engage in a complicated juggling act to provide a dynamic balance among the four Colors – the Four-P's. How can you create a common purpose with your children? How can you manage your daily life experiences so that you can focus on short-term needs without losing sight of long-term goals? How can you support your children's decision making parameters within the context of your own parameters? How can you help your children align their daily life experiences with a deep and abiding set of principles that are both personally rewarding and contribute in positive ways toward helping others? Finally, how can you help your children leverage available resources to achieve their own priorities.

Human Architectural Design

Human beings are resilient creatures. Most of us manage to interact with our fellow human beings with a reasonable amount of effectiveness. But you can increase your children's chances of effectiveness when you understand some fundamental principles of human architectural design. Figure 1.5 provides a general framework for **Real Colors®** architectural design.

Human Architectural Design
Figure 1.5

Understanding Real Colors® Architecture

Figure 1.5 illustrates how children learn and grow through their experiences. The top half of the figure refers to the connections that children make from one experience to another. The bottom half indicates how children tend to approach new experiences. Some children make strong connections from one experience to another based on how those experiences impact people *(top left picture)*. Other children make similarly strong connections based on how the experiences connect logically and consistently *(top right picture)*. Some children tend to engage in or avoid experiences according to their past experiences *(bottom left picture)*. And finally, some children are more willing to take risks by exploring new situations *(bottom right picture)*.

From infancy children learn that if they cry long enough and loud enough, they can attract their parents' attention. Based on these experiences, babies learn to enhance the probability that their actions will achieve expected results *(bottom left picture)*. However, as babies have more and more experiences, they get slightly different results from one experience to another. They learn that there are multiple ways to gain attention *(bottom right picture)*. In short, they learn that they can act either to increase their options or to narrow them to get what they want.

Children watch the people around them for clues about what draws approval or a sense of belonging *(top left picture)* and connect those clues into patterns of thought that explain human interactions *(top right picture)*. When babies cry long enough and loud enough, mom and dad are likely to give them what they want. But strangers may walk away. Within a very short time, children develop principles to regulate their behaviors according to their needs and their audience. They learn to analyze their actions and their results to determine how they want to allocate their efforts to meet future needs.

Again, both Paula and Lamberto and Janet and Luis, mentioned earlier, wanted to be good parents. Janet and Luis made decisions to establish a non-traditional family where Janet assumed a role as the main "bread winner" for the family while Luis assumed the role of homemaker. How will their choices both strengthen and create liabilities for their children?

How did Lamberto's past experiences get in the way of his relationship with his son, Paul? At first Lamberto thought Paul's antics were simply a part of growing up. "I was the same way when I was his age," Lamberto would tell Paula. "He'll outgrow this. I did. I would have outgrown it a lot sooner if my dad had been more understanding instead of being such a drill sergeant."

But when Paul stepped over the line by violating Lamberto's trust, they ended up in a tug of war to see who would determine the future course of Paul's life. What happens when parents forget that they are not building a house for themselves but for their children? Your children are not simply guests in your home. They did not accept an invitation to dinner that can easily be withdrawn. Creating a child involves a commitment, a relationship that does not end simply because it becomes strained.

Understanding Real Colors® Architecture

Before considering how you can broaden your parenting skills, take a moment to reflect on this chapter by responding to the items on the next several pages. As you reflect, think about how you might use these concepts and strategies to realize your dreams as a parent in ways that enhance your children's dreams as evolving human beings. Ask yourself the following questions:

Have we as parents...

1. *Developed a common commitment regarding our expectations for our children's growth and development?*

2. *Created avenues for our children to discuss their expectations for their lives and to make effective decisions according to their value structures?*

3. *Aligned our daily behaviors so that we model the principles underlying our stated values?*

4. *Made it possible for our children to act on their own priorities and to live with the consequences of their decisions?*

You cannot expect to develop these skills in your children overnight. Children need to be given increasing levels of responsibility as they learn and grow. But the messages you send through your behaviors start to form your children's attitudes at a very early age.

A Real Colors® Architectural Review

1. Place the Colors in the order of your own Color rainbow
   (Blue, Gold, Green, Orange).

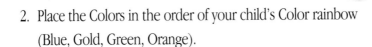

2. Place the Colors in the order of your child's Color rainbow
   (Blue, Gold, Green, Orange).

3. How did you arrive at your conclusions about your child's Color rainbow?

4. Use pictures or words to fill in the chart below so that it describes your human architectural plan for your child?

Goals	Parameters for Realizing Those Goals
Ways You Plan to Monitor Whose Goals Are Being Realized	**Ways You Will Decide Who Makes Which Decisions**

5. If your child is old enough (perhaps 10-12 years old), have him or her complete a similar chart.

Goals	Parameters for Realizing Those Goals

Ways You Plan to Monitor Whose Goals Are Being Realized	Ways You Will Decide Who Makes Which Decisions

6. How do the plans match up?

7. What are the unique challenges presented by the similarities and differences in these plans?

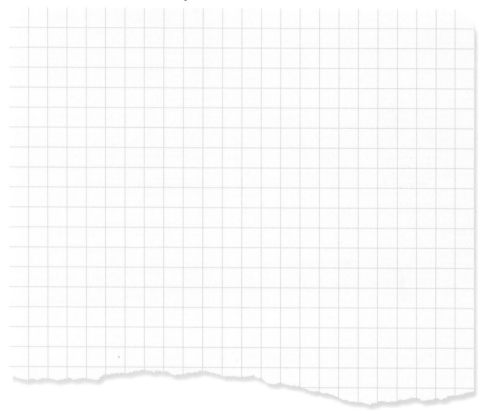

ASKING REAL COLORS® ARCHITECTURAL QUESTIONS

So you want to be a more effective parent. You have thought a great deal about **Real Colors®** architecture, and now you want to get started with your drawings. Before you break out the computer-assisted drawing program, however, let's return to Lamberto and Paul's relationship

from the last chapter. Where did it break down?

If you said before it got started, you would be absolutely correct. The parent-child relationship started to break down within the office of "Lamberto and Paula, Human Architects." You may recall that Lamberto and Paula had differences regarding the parameters that they would use to parent Paul. Lamberto wanted to give Paul his space while Paula wanted to pull in the reins. Effective parenting requires consistency within the architectural firm – between the father and the mother. Effective parenting requires more than "random acts of success." It requires a consistent set of plans and a consistent way of communicating those plans. How will you and your spouse as architectural partners bring the best of your parental skills to bear in developing architectural plans for your child's Color home?

The first step toward becoming an effective architectural firm lies in recognizing that you and your spouse may define effective parenting in different ways. The second step lies in recognizing these differences as assets rather than obstacles. If you approach your responsibilities openly and consistently, you can use your differences to expand opportunities for your children to grow.

In this chapter you will learn how to ask questions that identify your architectural strengths as a way of developing your child's *Color rainbow*. These questions can help you approach parenting as a growth opportunity for both you and your children. Notice how the factors of this partnership are outlined in Figure 2.1. This figure is an adaptation of a concept that educators use for building a sense of partnership or community in a school setting, but it works equally well for the human architectural firm (the parent-child partnership).

Notice that the focus of this chart is the growth and development of the child. If parents are going to be effective in designing growth opportunities for their children, they must be running in tandem toward common goals *(upper left picture)*. They must communicate *(upper right)* their own set of strengths that they bring to the architectural table and then provide avenues for their children to communicate their Color preferences. They must provide opportunities for collaboration and reflection *(lower right picture)* throughout the learning process so that they can adjust the designs to fit the needs of their customer *(center)*. Finally, parents cannot lose sight of the fact that their combined life experiences place them in a leadership and facilitation role *(lower left picture)*. They must design the opportunities for growth, particularly during the early years of a child's life, and then increasingly fade into the background as the child matures.

Building a Parenting Partnership
Figure 2.1

Adapted from: Lieberman and Grolnick (1997).

If you want to balance your view of **Real Colors**® architecture with the needs and interests of your customers (your children), you need to understand the values that drive them. And there is no better way to find out what your children value than to ask them.

Of course, young children may have difficulty expressing their ideas in terms that an adult can understand. But it would probably be safe to suggest that in all but a few situations where children have physiological problems, this inability to express ideas comes from a lack of experience rather than a lack of ability. With very young children it is necessary and appropriate for parent-architects to observe and interpret the child-homeowner's values. As you provide experiences for your children, watch what makes them happy – how much they seek security and comfort versus how much they seek risk and adventure. Remember, children do not have a stockpile of experiences to draw from. Their early years are a series of discoveries. Many of their daily experiences require them to take risks. It is a risk to leave the comfort of mom's arms, frightening to be alone and unable to fend for yourself, frustrating to want something that you cannot articulate, and dangerous to take a first step when you have little sense of balance or depth perception.

Whether you are asking the following questions of your older children or of yourself as you observe your younger children in multiple situations, they provide a lens through which you can begin to identify their Color rainbow – their strengths and liabilities. Again, I refer to these questions as the Four-P's (Johnson, 2005).

Purpose (Blue)	What is important for my child to know and be able to do?
Parameters (Gold)	What should we as parents know and be able to do in order to design opportunities for this kind of growth?
Principles (Green)	How will we adjust our designs as circumstances change?
Priorities (Orange)	How will we decide when our child can make the decisions and when we as parents should make them?

Purpose Questions

Effective architectural designs require a commitment to a shared purpose. This commitment runs deeper than spoken goals. A shared purpose runs to the heart of parent and child values. A commitment to a shared purpose is more a matter of understanding than rules. Let's assume that you want your child to take appropriate risks: walking, staying with grandparents or babysitters, going to pre-school, etc. Why might you approach this goal differently if your child's primary Color is Orange as opposed to Blue, Green, or Gold? To paint a clear target for both short-term and long-term success, parents need to help children understand their strengths before helping them overcome their liabilities.

Be ever vigilant about interpreting your children's behaviors or direct

answers to questions from your own frame of reference. When Blue parents hear an answer to a "purpose" question, they may want to move forward while everyone is in agreement. When Gold parents hear an answer to a "purpose" question, they may want to create rules and procedures that ensure consistent expectations for compliance. Green parents may want to create a plan to monitor progress, and Orange parents may want to move immediately to action. The parental listener's guide in Figure 2.2 illustrates how you can train yourself to listen to your child's answer rather than for the answer you want to hear.

A Parental Listener's Guide

Figure 2.2

Response	Purpose response to a purpose response	Parameters response to a purpose response	Principles response to a purpose response	Priorities response to a purpose response
	From these…			
Four responses to a purpose question	We agree, and I know you can do it.	Okay, then let's agree on the rules for…	But how will we know that you are sticking to this plan?	I don't think that is nearly as important as…
	To these…			
A slight twist to keep the focus on quality	I agree, but what does that look like to you?	That sounds interesting. Can you tell us what you would be doing if this plan works?	I can see your point. How can we check in with each other to make certain you have any help you need?	That sounds exciting, but are you certain that this is more important to you than…?

To a Blue, rules and procedures require people to do something as opposed to developing a natural commitment to a shared purpose. Blues sometimes see Green monitoring processes as communicating a lack of trust or getting in the way of "what really matters." They worry that forcing choices on children might stifle their creativity.

1. *How will we know if our plan is working?*
2. *How have we made things like this work in the past?*
3. *How will we make certain that everyone gets a chance to choose a favorite activity?*
4. *Who will decide when we need to change our plan?*

These questions shift the focus from what we want to what we can make work. While the answers may differ from one situation to another, they will help architects and their customers (parents and children) focus on a common purpose or target.

Parameters Questions

Parameters questions help children paint the target. They define a set of standards that help children determine what it is they are trying to accomplish and how they will know when they have been successful. Parameters questions help children (and their parents for that matter) manage the multiple factors involved in most real-life situations. They also demonstrate to children that not every factor of every situation can be controlled, that the best solutions sometimes give way to manageable solutions.

Seven-year-old Tommy and his parents sat down to discuss Tommy's  behavior in school. Tommy was a shy child at home, but his teacher had reported that he was acting out on the playground: bullying other children and refusing to allow others to play in his group. Tommy's parents might have expected this behavior from their older son, Chad. But unlike his restless and competitive Orange brother, Tommy always seemed to be more of a peace keeping Blue.

When Gloria and Jack sat down with Tommy, they asked several questions.

Shy Tommy and the Playground Bully

❝ Tommy, can you tell us what the problem is at school?" Gloria asked.

"I don't think Mrs. Ortega likes me anymore," Tommy mumbled, holding back a stream of tears.

"Why do you say that?" Jack asked.

"Because she told me she was very disappointed in me and that you and mom would be too. She said I was certainly not the good kid I was at the start of school. I think she likes Bobby Thomas more than me."

"I doubt that, but what makes you think so?" Gloria asked.

"Chad said so. He said that Mrs. Ortega never liked him and she probably was going to start picking on me now. I don't get it. Chad told me I needed to stick up for myself so the other kids wouldn't call me a sissy."

It was becoming clear to Jack and Gloria that their Blue first grader was getting mixed messages from his Orange fifth grade brother. After some brief consultations with one another in which Jack and Gloria brought his Orange and her Blue to bear on the situation, they brought their two sons together for another discussion.

"Chad, were you aware that Tommy was having some problems on the playground at school?" asked Gloria.

"Yea, I even told him how to handle them. But Mrs. Ortega seems to be taking out her dislike for me on Tommy," Chad responded.

"Well, that could be, I suppose," said Jack. "But she certainly gave you a lot of chances when you were in first grade. And you said she always goes out of her way to speak to you at the park or in the grocery store."

"I know. It's confusing, isn't it?" suggested Chad.

"You know, Chad, I think you were trying to help Tommy with his problem, but have your solutions gotten you into more or less trouble at school?" asked Gloria.

"More, I guess."

"Well, where do you think we should go from here, boys?" asked Jack.

See how the story concludes on the next page!

"I could tell Mrs. Ortega and the kids I'm sorry and just go back to acting like myself again," said Tommy.

"And I could go with him to tell Mrs. Ortega I'm sorry too and tell her that I was trying to get that Bobby Thomas to leave Tommy alone," added Chad.

"That sounds like a good plan," said Gloria, "and how will we know if it's working?"

"Maybe we need to have Mrs. Ortega send you a note each week to let you know how I'm doing," said Tommy.

"And what should the note say if things are improving?" asked Jack.

"That I'm being like I was at the beginning of the year," offered Tommy.

"And that I'm not meddling in Tommy's business at school," added Chad sheepishly.

"Sounds like a plan," said Gloria. "I'll call Mrs. Ortega tomorrow afternoon to make certain we are all on the same page."

Jack and Gloria could have saved time and energy by simply reprimanding both boys for their behavior. They could have told them their expectations for their behavior. But they recognized a chance to turn a negative situation into a positive learning opportunity for both Tommy and Chad. By taking a little extra time, they accomplished the following:

- *Allowing both boys an opportunity to express the reasons behind their actions.*

- *Helping both boys assume responsibility for the problem as well as for the solution.*

- *Steering the boys through a reflective process regarding their behavior.*

- *Helping them set a clear target for successful resolution of the problem.*

- *Providing ongoing monitoring and support by setting a time when Gloria would contact Mrs. Ortega.*

Growth and development is about changing more than behaviors. It is about building a child's reflection and problem solving skills. It is about helping children build on their own strengths. We all think about purpose, parameters, principles, and priorities at some point during our daily experiences. But we tend to focus on one of the four questions more than the other three. To become an effective parent, you need to help your children develop what Quinn (1996) calls "deep change," change that runs beyond behaviors to attitudes. Your children are more likely to change their behaviors once they have changed their attitudes. When they share responsibilities for defining success, they begin to recognize that their parents' ideas can strengthen rather than detract from their goals.

It is apparent that Jack and Gloria's questions imply an expectation for change. The quality of the questions determines how successful the change process will be. Jack and Gloria's purpose defines their vision of growth for both Tommy and Chad. Their purpose becomes the standard against which they measure their effectiveness as parents. You can use questions like Jack and Gloria's to help your children paint a personal target for success.

Principle Questions

I refer to questions that help people solve problems as critical questions. Critical questions elevate the level of conversation between parents and children. They shift the focus from a simple right or wrong to degrees of success – success for whom – the child; under what conditions – those that you and they have worked on together; given what evidence – again, the standards for success that you help them set. Critical questions engage children in improving their own situation. They learn that they have the ability to solve their own problems, and this gives them a sense of control over their own lives. They become problem solvers rather than victims.

It is important for parents to remember that they are the architects who provide guidance to their children's plans for building their own Color home. Effective architects ask questions and listen carefully for the values implied in their customer's responses. This is not a process that happens overnight. And you should not assume that because your children exercise problem solving skills in one situation that they can apply them with equal skill or success under even a seemingly similar set of circumstances.

Marzano et al. (2001) indicates that it is very important for adults to help children recognize similarities and differences from one situation or event to another. They also suggest that children should be encouraged to summarize what they have learned. Asking your children to summarize what they have learned helps them organize their thinking and provides opportunities for you to help them clarify cause and effect relationships within a situation.

Gold parents tend to define success in terms of working hard and following the rules. Hard work is a necessary part of success, as is an ability to follow the rules. However, these skills are only part of the overall set of skills that children will need to navigate their way through life. They need to learn how to remain open for the right opportunity (Orange), to recognize when all the work in the world may not move a brick wall (Green), and to understand when hard work directed toward the wrong short-term purpose (Blue) can actually be counterproductive to accomplishing their long-term goals.

And problem solving opportunities for children should not always be focused on "fixing" a situation. When Annie and Chuck, along with Chuck's 14 year-old son, Joey, were discussing the possibility of purchasing a dog, each one had a different idea of what the ideal animal would look like. Annie wanted a small dog, Joey wanted a large dog, and Chuck wasn't certain any

of them had the time to take care of a dog of any size or breed. Suddenly Annie asked, "What is the purpose of this discussion? Why did we even begin it?"

Chuck said that he thought it all started with the idea of having something that brought the three of them closer together since Joey was Annie's stepson and had not lived with Chuck since he was six years-old. After some laughter and a few awkward moments, they agreed that this had been the purpose. Then Annie said, "And what are the parameters that each of us has to live with if this is going to work? How will we hold one another accountable for the care of the dog? And how will we make certain that we all have fun shopping for this addition to our family?"

Critical questions should focus on your children's needs and should communicate your desire to help them achieve their goals. Remember, these critical questions model the type of learning that you want to encourage in your children. Therefore, don't always apply them to situations in which you think you already know the "correct" answer. Be willing to learn and discover with your children. Don't be afraid to be wrong. Otherwise, your children will come to see such questions as merely an adult trick to manipulate their thinking.

Approximately three out of four children will be first order concrete thinkers (Gold or Orange) who may need help seeing connections between and among situations. Approximately one in five (Blues) will probably see the connections between people's feelings and the situation at hand. Fewer than one in ten will immediately notice the connections from one situation to the next (Green). Those children (Blues and Greens) who are most likely to see the connections, on the other hand, may have difficulty arriving at conclusions (Golds) or may be hesitant to act (Orange).

As a parent it is your responsibility to understand your children's strengths and to help them fill in the gaps. Don't tell them your answer. Help them discover their answer. It is both correct and responsible as a parent to determine how much decision making your children are capable of handling. But be certain to ask yourself whom you are protecting: you or your children.

Do your children have opportunities to solve their own problems? Or do you only allow them that freedom when you know what their answer will be? Is the answer right for them or designed to win your approval? Are you willing to think critically, and do you practice this skill regularly as an adult? If not, you are probably not modeling critical thinking for your children. Parenting is a tough balancing act between protecting your children and giving them reasonable opportunities to grow.

Neither the closed world of givens nor its counterpart of no guidelines whatsoever provides the full skill set that you will need to become an effective parent. Ask yourself how you can provide a balance between discovery and exploration, a balance between values and standards. Your children need opportunities to think critically and creatively so that they can explore new and better solutions to real life problems.

Where should the target be placed now and how will we decide when to move it at some time in the future? The answer to this question implies the need for parents to consider their children's maturity, their level of experience, and the risks involved in a particular situation. Well, no one said parenting was going to be easy.

Solving problems requires access to information. As a parent you wonder how much information, how much guidance, etc. you will need to provide. There are no easy answers to these questions. Access involves far more than knowing what is going on. It involves knowing the implications of what is going on. Access questions require you to consider not only the impact on your children, but the impact on other people's children if your children decide to share their newly discovered information. Your children may be mature enough to deal with the new information. But are they mature enough to know when and with whom to share it?

For example, did you notice in the earlier example when Jack and Gloria helped Tommy and Chad solve their problem at school that they did not comment on Bobby Thomas' behavior? Instead, they kept the focus on what they could manage (parameters) in terms of their own family. They allowed Chad to suggest that Tommy's teacher, Mrs. Ortega, might be picking on Tommy because she "disliked Chad." Then Jack asked Chad to think about evidence that might suggest a contrary conclusion. By helping Chad reach his own conclusions, Jack avoided any opportunity for Chad to suggest an adult conspiracy of teacher and parents against Tommy and himself.

Ten-year-old Chad, probably more so than 7-year-old Tommy, was making connections relevant to fundamental issues of principle – how to solve his problems without negatively impacting others, thinking about the conse-quences of his own actions and the consequences of giving poor advice to his younger brother. But even Tommy had to summarize his problem's solution and establish standards for measuring its effectiveness.

Let's think about critical questions for a moment. What should they do?

Characteristics of Critical Questions

- *Require all those involved to reflect on the same information.*
- *Include goal setting, making a plan, implementing that plan, monitoring the situation, and adjusting the plan if necessary to achieve the desired results.*
- *Provide "early warning" signals so that parents and children know what extra effort might be necessary.*
- *Clarify who is accountable for what.*
- *Create a timely, practical reporting process.*

What is your picture for becoming a more effective parent? How are you doing with critical questions? Are you modeling questioning as a life-long process or simply as something that children learn to do to please their parents? Have you ever involved your children in solving one of your problems, or are you sending the message that adults already have all the answers to life's problems?

Priorities Questions

The key to growth is not how much information you and your children can amass, but how you act on it. Marzano (2003) suggests that adults can help children "try out" their skills by following the three steps listed below:

1. *Provide timely feedback on specific actions (Tommy's letters from Mrs. Ortega and Gloria's phone call to Mrs. Ortega).*

2. *Establish specific, challenging achievement goals (Gloria's question to Tommy and Chad about how they would know if they were successful).*

3. Establish specific goals for each child (both Tommy and Chad had to do something as a result of the family's problem solving session).

You can help your children to...

- *Identify their personal expectations.*
- *Compare their expectations with one another and with you.*

When you...

- *Ask open-ended questions that clarify conflicting expectations.*
- *Listen to their answers rather than for the answers you expect.*
- *Keep your focus on what you want your children to learn rather than what you need to prove.*

Effective priorities questions go beyond results. They help your children establish a set of underlying principles that connect factors related to one situation or problem into an overall picture of growth and development. Parents need to help their children "find success and replicate it." By focusing on success you create a positive, safe environment where your children will become more willing to consider how they can use their strengths to overcome their liabilities. It is important for you to consider how you can enhance your children's opportunities for success so that they develop a healthy attitude toward accountability – how they are meeting their obligations to themselves and to others.

A simple listing of successes will not be enough to convince your children that they need to invest more time and energy in problem solving. If you fail to make the Four-P's a natural and fun process, it will not become meaningful or manageable for them. Credible parents communicate values as much through their actions as through their words. Remember, your children will pay attention to those things that have a direct and compelling impact on their lives.

Parents need time to live with and reflect on newly attained skills before they can apply them or pass them onto their children. It may be a good idea for you and your spouse to apply the Four-P's to your own problem situations before trying to pass them onto your children. Take the time to evaluate your own skills. This may help you think about how your own strengths and liabilities as a problem solver may enhance or limit your ability to teach these skills to your children. What strengths does your Color rainbow bring to your parenting responsibilities? What does your spouse's Rainbow add to your strengths? Do your combined strengths (your combined primary and secondary Colors) cover all of the Four-P's, or do you still have some Colors missing?

When you recognize your liabilities, you can communicate why all people need to set priorities. No person is good at everything, and even the best problem solvers can only manage so many factors at any one time. There are numerous ways to solve problems, each with its own set of advantages and disadvantages. Chicksynmihayl (1990) suggests that people are most likely to feel a sense of success when they know how to set realistic goals that match their skills appropriately to the situation at hand. You can help your children develop this set of skills that Chicksynmihayl calls "flow" by helping them limit the scope of their problem solving efforts to fit their level of maturity, by providing feedback, and by celebrating each small success with them.

Asking Real Colors® Architectural Questions

Child growth and development is a qualitative rather than a compliance issue. Piaget (1977) suggests that children learn by dealing with some degree of dissonance between what they already believe and what they confront in new situations. But Hart (1983) reminds us that when children are placed in a situation that becomes too threatening, they can see themselves as helplessness victims. Therefore, quality growth opportunities for your children depend on your ability to ask them questions that make their tasks more manageable. You can help them understand that success is a moving target.

Parents cannot simply declare a change in their own or their children's attitudes or behaviors. To become a more effective parent, you may need to change your concept of how children learn. Remember that while you and your children use the same Four-P's to solve problems, you don't necessarily use them in the same order.

You cannot change your children's personalities, but you can use key questions to help them focus their thinking. Questions focused on the Four-P's promote balance and enhance opportunities for success. As your children see their ideas in action and see that they have the ability to solve problems, they will gain a better sense of how and when they need to move their growth target to the next level.

Children learn by engaging with their world and making various connections between and among their experiences. Learning is about making connections with people and ideas, connections that provide both the means and the ends of learning. The more you and your children practice the Four-P's and compare the results of your experiences with one another, the more effective you will both become as learners. By understanding personality differences, your children can learn to thrive on differences rather than avoiding them.

It is impossible for parents to determine whether their children are being beautifully and necessarily different or arbitrarily difficult. But unless you can give them a voice in determining the direction of their own growth and development, they will have little incentive to become thoughtful problem solvers. After all, it is much easier initially for children to follow their parents' advice. That way if things don't work out as planned, your children can blame you. But by providing opportunities for them to participate in their own problem solving with your guidance and support, you can encourage them to take more responsibility for their actions.

How will you leverage your strengths to promote success for your children? How will you help your children develop a habit of asking the Four-P questions? In the next chapter we will consider several strategies that you can use to make the Four-P questions a habit in your home. But before moving to these strategies, take a moment to consider what questions you are currently asking your children.

Asking Better Architectural Questions

1. How often do I sit down with my children to have a discussion about their daily lives?

2. How well do my questions address the Four-P's? (List one or two questions under each of the Four-P's that you have recently asked your children.)

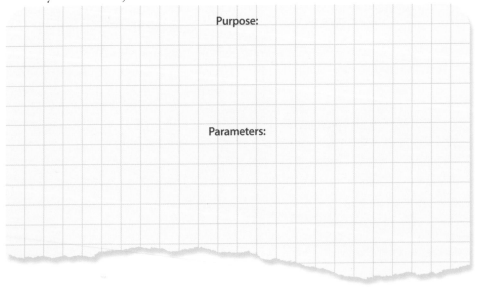

Purpose:

Parameters:

Asking Real Colors® Architectural Questions

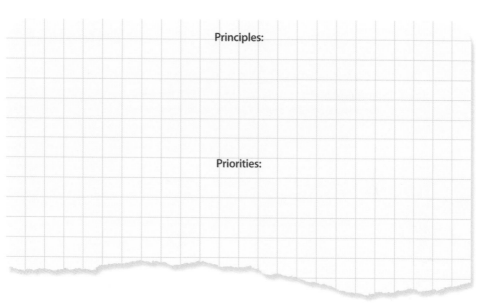

Principles:

Priorities:

3. To what extent have I thought of my children's problems as growth opportunities for them and for myself as a parent?

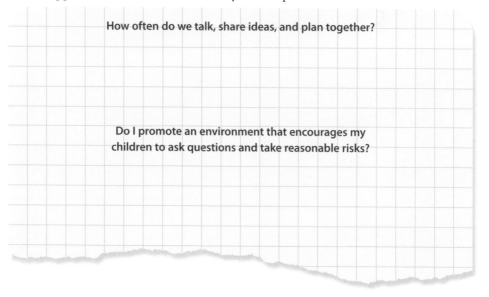

How often do we talk, share ideas, and plan together?

Do I promote an environment that encourages my children to ask questions and take reasonable risks?

4. My preparation and implementation plans for asking better questions are as follows:

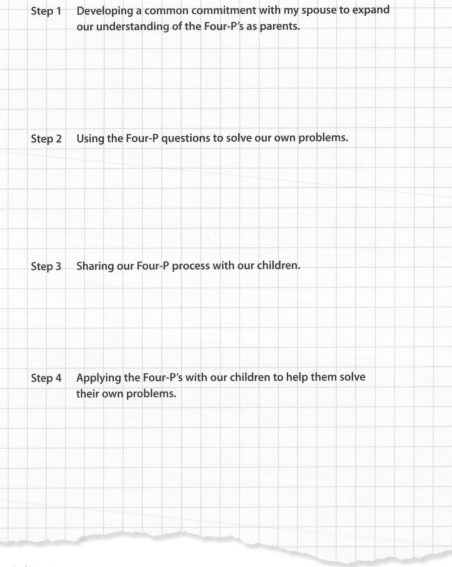

Step 1   Developing a common commitment with my spouse to expand our understanding of the Four-P's as parents.

Step 2   Using the Four-P questions to solve our own problems.

Step 3   Sharing our Four-P process with our children.

Step 4   Applying the Four-P's with our children to help them solve their own problems.

Asking Real Colors® Architectural Questions

5. What is my development/implementation timeline?

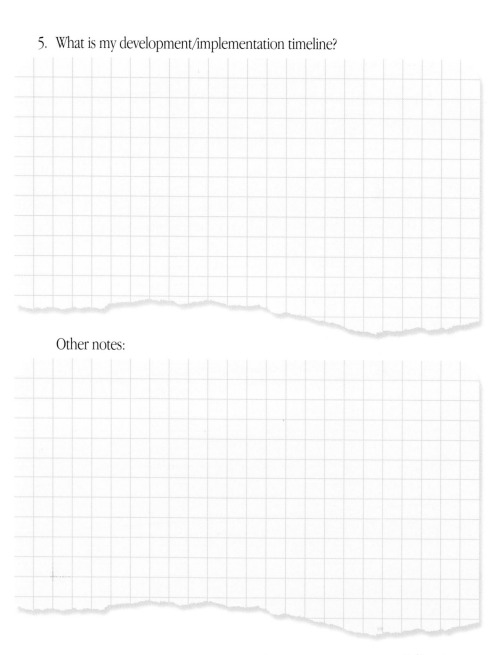

Other notes:

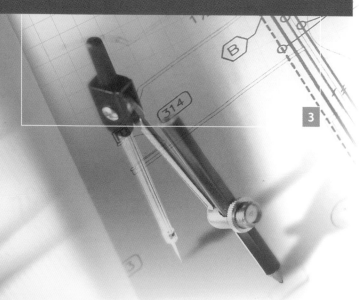

PLANS, SCHEMATICS AND BUILDING CODES

3

Plans, Schematics, and Building Codes

Have you ever driven through an established neighborhood where the houses had a rich history and a sense of comfort? If these homes are well kept and accessible to transportation routes, they can be very expensive to purchase. But when people buy such homes, they often find that they require a great deal of renovation in order to meet the demands of current life-style expectations. That wrap-around front porch may need new floorboards, the high ceilings and old windows may make heating expensive, and the old wiring and plumbing may not be adequate for today's appliances. As a potential homeowner you may decide that you cannot afford to live in such a neighborhood, that the lure of old-fashion values is outweighed by the costs of remodeling. You may decide to look for something more modern and less expensive.

Next you drive through a neighborhood where homes are new and less expensive. There are still some available lots where you could build your own home. As you drive along, you notice that every home in this neighborhood looks the same. You could afford the houses here, and they are brand new. But you had your sights set on a two-story, and all these houses are ranches. After looking into the local homeowner's association rules, you learn that you cannot build a two-story home in this development.

Parenting is often a very similar experience. How are you approaching your role as a human architect? Are you determined to design a Color home for your child that resembles the one that your parents designed for you? Or do you think that you can create a better design? Have you watched other parents design Color homes for their children? Have you found those

Plans, Schematics, and Building Codes

homes lacking in quality, in beauty, or in functionality? Are you determined to create a better design, to create a Color home that is the envy of the neighborhood?

Many parents are determined to repair the ills of society (or at least the ills of their childhood) by raising a perfect child. While it is fine to hold high architectural standards for child rearing, you may want to ask how different you want your child's Color home to look. You may want to ask yourself how your design criteria fit with community building codes. How unique can your child's Color home design be before it becomes bizarre? Don't forget that the rules of the game change when your child steps beyond the family confines.

This dilemma demonstrates the difference between honesty and integrity. According to Warren Bennis (1989) honesty comes from setting a goal and trying to follow it (walking your talk). Integrity comes from setting goals that reflect the way you live your life (talking your walk). When you talk your walk, you model the behaviors and attitudes you want your children to exhibit – as opposed to "do as I say, not as I do."

It is not enough to ask your children the right questions if you are not going to adjust your architectural plans accordingly. It is not enough to draw plans without thinking about engineering schematics. And the best architectural plans and engineering schematics will mean little if the house you are designing does not meet local building codes.

Plans, Schematics, and Building Codes

You can help your child design a comfortable Color home, but you cannot do it in a vacuum. Your child has expectations for this home, you have expectations, and the community has expectations as well. How might you use the following questions to coordinate those expectations?

- *Do my child and I have a commitment to a common purpose?*
- *Do we have equal access to information?*
- *How often do we collaborate and reflect on our plans?*
- *How can a parent-architect lead and facilitate this planning?*

Adapted from Leiberman and Grolnick (1997).

Why Have A Plan?

Golds are not comfortable when something they value does not work. Blues are not comfortable when the people around them are unhappy. Greens are not comfortable when the people around them aren't thinking logically. Oranges are not comfortable when the events of their day aren't challenging and exciting. Regardless of your Color order, you have developed expectations for yourself and others. But as a parent you must let go of these expectations enough to allow your child's expectations to emerge in a healthy manner.

This chapter describes how you can create architectural plans and engineering schematics that meet or exceed community building codes. Agreeing to a goal is different from developing a commitment to a shared purpose. Again, to commit to a shared purpose, you and your child must agree on what your goals look like in action. You need to agree on the target and on your expectations for hitting the target. That is, what kind of Color home are you trying to create and what are the behaviors that you should expect from one another if you are hitting the target on a regular basis?

The chances are somewhere between one and two in ten that shared purpose will be your normal entry point for parenting. Remember, only 10-15% of the world's population is Blue. While most parents want to believe that they have a shared purpose with their children in developing their course in life, chances are almost one in two that you will have very specific expectations for your child's behaviors and attitudes. (Golds comprise 45-50% of the world's parents.) Even with the best of intentions many Gold parents make the assumption that their non-Gold children's "misbehaviors" are simply examples of their not listening to directions or practicing enough.

Or are you one of the 35-40% of parents who believe that the best way to teach your children to swim is to throw them into the pool? Orange parents believe that doing something is better than doing nothing at all. Do you become frustrated when your child doesn't get it the first time? Do you want to make certain that your children can "stand on their own two feet?" Do you push them to participate and encourage them to excel?

Or are you one of the fewer than 5% of parents who are Green? Do you study childcare books, worrying that your child might not be measuring up? Do you overwhelm your children with questions and stifle them with planning and detailed explanations?

As we discussed in *The Homeowner's Guide*, few parents stay awake at night conjuring up ways to make their children's lives miserable. And

Plans, Schematics, and Building Codes

child-rearing "mistakes" are not always a factor of parents being at odds with their children. Angel, a high school math teacher, expresses it this way, *"Who is to say that one method of parenting is better than another? After all, there really is no certification for being a parent. Kids appreciate discipline. They want limitations. I think it is simply a matter of common sense – don't you?"*

There is nothing inherently wrong with Angel's position. In fact, when she stated it at a community meeting, most of her friends agreed with her. Her friend, Emily, adds, "I agree. My mother and father felt that as long as I lived in their house, I would go to church every Sunday and attend youth fellowship. If I got into trouble at school, I was in even more trouble at home. They never asked me if I wanted to take piano or dance lessons. It was simply an expectation. And I don't think it hurt me one bit. I think parents today spend too much time explaining things to kids. When I see my sister-in-law with her kids, I wonder who is in charge."

"I know exactly what you mean," their friend Yoko chimes in. "My parents and I used to argue all the time when I was a teenager. Now that I realize how difficult raising children can be, I regret all those sleepless nights I must have caused my parents. Parenting is a heavy responsibility. It requires a lot of hard work."

Plans, Schematics, and Building Codes

So if it is not my fault as a parent, whose fault is it? Our kids deserve better. "Why doesn't the school district…? With all the violence on television…? With all the peer pressure today…?" And when we have a premise regarding blame, we typically turn to others who believe as we believe to reinforce our position.

Golds find support from one another. To Golds the "problem" lies with those parents who simply don't care. How can we protect our children from all the temptations that confront them today when other parents simply turn their heads the other way? When effective parenting strategies (my perception, of course) do not yield the desirable results, something or someone must be working against me.

Blues find support from other Blues. Together these purpose driven people lament the situation. Perhaps it is not that no one cares, but that everyone is just too busy trying to earn a living in this fast-paced world. People mean well, but there is just too much violence in the world. If only people could come together, reach out for some higher purpose…

Greens, though solitary, look to one another to verify their analyses of the problem. They see people working harder instead of working smarter. They are incredulous at the lack of logical thinking that permeates the world around them. They wonder aloud why people cannot see the obvious answers all around them just waiting to be discovered.

Oranges seek one another for release from all the rules, all the crazy habits that get in the way of people trying to get the job done. They find entertaining pastimes for release from all the lamenting around them. They marvel that people seem to care more about how the problem "might" be solved rather than rolling up their sleeves and getting to work.

If all these folks are "a little bit right" in their thinking, then why is it that they can't agree on a common solution? Why can't they set aside their differences, or better yet, use those differences to reach a common purpose? Several years ago a ten-year-old boy named Josh answered this question for me more succinctly than anyone else I have heard tackle it before or since. "You see," he said, "a liability is nothing more than a strength you carry too far." And herein lies the problem. Agreement is not about accepting another person's premise. It is about how much you accept it. And it is not simply how much you accept the premise, but how you deal with the premise once you find agreement.

The right tools...

My son, Joel, and I are both Greens. We should agree, right? Well, we typically agree on how problems should be analyzed and on what factors should be taken into consideration during that analysis process. Where we often risk disagreement, however, is in what we do with the information once we agree on a "truth." As a Green-Gold, Joel relies on the tools he knows and understands. That is, he pulls the tools from his toolbox and gets immediately to work — solve this problem according to the methods used in the past to solve similar problems. I, on the other hand, am a Green-Orange. I don't always assume that the tools necessary to fix the problem have been invented yet. If they already exist, why hasn't someone solved this problem? Will our tendency be to agree or to disagree? The answer to that question is not black or white. It is a matter of degree.

Is there a right tool?

My other son, Sean, is a Blue-Orange. He sees most problems as simply a matter of misunderstanding. He wants first to feel good about the people with whom he is working. He wants to believe that ultimately they have the same purpose in mind that he has. That's his Blue showing. Then he says, "Who is to say what is right or wrong? If they are not hurting anyone, why do we care what they do – Orange?"

Who's right here? Who's wrong? How right is each person? I like myself and think both my sons are good people. Can they both be right? If they are right, am I wrong? Or as ten-year-old Josh says, "Perhaps a liability is nothing more than a strength carried too far." Our behaviors are often the result of our habits, attitudes, and values. Let's take a look at how we can help our children develop habits based on their strengths without turning them into liabilities. That is, how can we act as architects, understanding that we are helping our children design their homes, not the homes we would want them to have if they were "more like us."

House Plans: Helping Children Develop Habits That Work For Them

Actually there is no way for our children to avoid their liabilities unless we try to turn them into someone other than themselves. What we can do is to help them understand and accept how they think and act naturally – what works for them. As we considered in the last chapter, the best way to find out what people believe is to ask them good questions. And whether we are working with very young children or with adolescents, we need to observe their actions to be certain whether they are sharing their true beliefs and values or telling us what they think we want/expect to hear.

Infants and young children live in an Orange world. Their lives are about exploration and discovery. Therefore, if parents want to see their children's **Real Colors**®, they must observe their children and listen to their questions and answers. Do they act first and then ask questions, or do they ask questions before they act? Do they ask why bad things happened to them and rely on your explanation, or do they ask for your opinion and then argue with your response? Do they act first and ask for forgiveness, or do they seek your permission before they act? These are all key questions that you can ask yourself as you observe your children. But what are the questions you can ask them to gain a better understanding of their Color rainbow, and when should you ask such questions?

As a middle school principal, I often schooled adolescents on when and how to ask questions. Never ask a teacher what you did wrong immediately after being reprimanded – even if you don't know what you did. Find a time when you are not the center of negative attention, a time when you are not perceived as posing a challenge. Watch the tone of your question. First, ask a question without stating your opinion. *"The other day when you were so upset with me, I thought I knew what I did wrong, but Joey said you were more upset with me for something else. Can you tell me for certain what I did wrong so that I don't get into trouble again?"* Then even if you think

Plans, Schematics, and Building Codes

the teacher was wrong, you can say, *"Oh, I see now why you would have been so upset with me. I'm sorry that it appeared that way to you. What I meant to say was…"*

The advice I gave those adolescents then is equally useful to parents today. Misbehavior cannot always go unnoticed. If Johnny broke the lamp as a result of wrestling in the living room after being told not to do that, you are more than justified as a parent to scold him. You would also be justified in requiring Johnny to pay for replacing the lamp. But then you must ask yourself whose problem you want to solve, whose house you are designing – your house or your child's house. Knowing what he did wrong is not necessarily going to help Johnny avoid a similar action in the future. Johnny probably won't wrestle in the living room when he grows up. He did not set out to break the lamp, and even the cost of replacing it may not be enough to change his habit of wrestling. In this case, Johnny's parents need to help him separate his behavior from this particular situation so that they can focus on his habits.

Sue and Tyrell are Johnny's parents. Having observed him daily for all of his ten years, they recognize that he is Orange. They realize that every day for Johnny represents a new adventure. When Johnny was very young, Sue and Tyrell had worried that he might have ADD (Attention Deficit Disorder). But their pediatrician assured them that Johnny was a normal little boy with an abundance of curiosity – and energy. By the time Johnny was six-years-old, he had broken both arms – his left arm three times. Having been a bit of a risk taker himself, Tyrell decided that he needed to get Johnny involved in a youth wrestling program to channel his energy in a positive direction. Tyrell and Sue agreed that they were not interested in creating an Olympian. They simply wanted Johnny to have a positive outlet for what had turned out to be a natural talent. Johnny practiced wrestling religiously. He watched it on television, insisted on going to wrestling matches at the local high school, and was always disappointed when youth wrestling season ended.

When Johnny broke the lamp in their living room, Sue was angry. She had talked with him several times about wrestling in the living room. Prior to the lamp debacle, Tyrell had even grounded Johnny for a week when he knocked over a cup of coffee on the coffee table as a result of wrestling with a friend in the living room. The broken lamp was almost the last straw. But then Tyrell decided to try another approach. He and Sue had attended a **Real Colors**® workshop and had been fascinated with the Colors concepts. They had read *The Real Colors Homebuilder's Guide* and decided to try out some of the Color strategies with Johnny. Tyrell and Johnny's conversation went as follows.

Plans, Schematics, and Building Codes

Wrestling Johnny and the Broken Lamp

"Johnny, what do you think we should do about this wrestling problem and the broken lamp?

"I told mom I would pay for it."

"Do you think that is enough to make up for the loss of that lamp. It was an antique, you know. It belonged to mom's great-grand-mother. It had special meaning to her."

"I suppose since I broke that special lamp, I should give up wrestling."

"Give up wrestling? You don't need to give up wrestling. But what could you do so that you don't break things in the house?"

"I could quit wrestling in the house, but since mom lost something very special to her, I should lose something very special to me so that I can learn a lesson."

"Well, I think you have learned a lesson already. You do feel bad about what you did, don't you?"

"Yes, I feel bad, but maybe wrestling is becoming a bad habit for me. Like mom said, this isn't the first time I've broken something in the house when I've been wrestling."

"Well, you know what? I don't think that your bad habit is wrestling. In fact, I think that is a good habit. You love it, and you're good at it."

"Yea, but it gets me into trouble here at home and at school. Maybe it's becoming a bad habit."

"Tell you what, Champ. I don't think wrestling is your bad habit. I think your bad habit might be acting before you think. But where is that a good habit in wrestling?"

"When I'm on my back on the mat?"

"That's right. Why is that a good time to act first?"

"On the mat I just seem to know what to do."

"You do what comes naturally to you. Because you don't have to think about a move before you execute it, you are faster than your opponents and you win a lot of wrestling matches. Any sport is more fun when you win. What you need to do is to develop some safety valves to let you make certain that wrestling is a way to get positive attention rather than negative attention."

See how the story concludes on the next page!

Plans, Schematics, and Building Codes

"But how do I do that?"

"Tell me where it is okay to wrestle."

"In the gym?"

"Sure. Any place else?"

"No."

"Could you wrestle in the basement?"

"Mom says no because I broke my arm when I fell on the concrete floor."

"I was thinking that if we had a mat down there, the basement might be a good place to wrestle when you are at home."

"Sure, that would be great."

"Wait a minute. Slow down. Let's talk about what we can learn here?"

"That there is a place to wrestle and a place not to wrestle."

"What makes a place a good place to wrestle? What should be in that place and what should not be there?'

"The place should be big enough to put a mat, and there shouldn't be any furniture or things that might break nearby."

"Okay, and what do you need to do about your thinking before you wrestle? What questions could you ask that would help you keep from hurting yourself or hurting someone else or something that belongs to someone else?"

(Johnny hesitates before responding. . .)

"If every time you were ready to wrestle you asked these questions, would it help: Where am I? Is there proper equipment to protect me

*from hurting myself or someone else? Is there anything breakable
nearby? Is there anything going on here that I will be interrupting?"*
"I could do that."
*"Johnny, these are questions that you can ask before a wrestling match
or when the urge hits you to wrestle at school or at home. If you get
into the habit of asking these four simple questions even before you
wrestle at practice or at a match – every time you wrestle – you will
be developing a habit that will make wrestling a way to get positive
recognition rather than negative recognition. What most people don't
understand is that our habits usually come from doing something we
enjoy. But we need to enjoy them in ways that don't interfere with
what other people enjoy. Now what are those four questions?"*

Tyrell realized that punishment was not working. Although it would have
changed Johnny's behavior for a time, the pleasure drawn from wrestling
clearly overpowered Johnny's desire to please his parents and teachers.
Tyrell could have forbidden Johnny from wrestling for a period of time,
but he recognized that his pent-up energy would likely show itself in some
other form or place such as school.

Most habits are engrained in us. They often result from something we
do well or that gives us the pleasure we are seeking. It is often difficult to
overcome "bad" habits because their origin lies within something we do
well or find pleasure in. Or perhaps they are a result of protecting our good
habits (what we enjoy) from those who prevent us from enjoying them.
This is what makes "bad" habits so hard to break. Liabilities (bad habits)
are nothing more than strengths (good habits) that we carry too far.

Plans, Schematics, and Building Codes

Sue and Tyrell took the time to consider whose house was being constructed here. Their physical house was being dismantled on a regular basis, but they were more focused on helping Johnny build his Color home. They saw a solution to Johnny's Color home plans as a potential solution to the well-being of their living room. They took the time to ask the parent-architect questions:

- *Do my child and I have a commitment to a common purpose?*
- *Do we have equal access to information?*
- *How often do we collaborate and reflect on our plans?*
- *How can a parent-architect lead and facilitate this planning?*

So in an age where many families don't sit down to a family meal, when do discussions like Tyrell had with Johnny take place? If you can't manage to have nightly meals as a family, can you have family meals two or three nights each week? If family members' schedules don't allow a common mealtime, can you set aside other common family times? My Mormon neighbors hold family meetings each week to talk about their daily lives and to support one another on a day-to-day basis. Can you find an hour per week to talk with your family members? It could pay real dividends. Sue and Tyrell could have solved their problem about the broken lamp by simply punishing Johnny. But they realized that they were creating a design for Johnny's Color home, not their own. They could do this because they have more knowledge than Johnny has about how the world works and what happens when you ignore social standards (local building codes). They knew that it was more important for Johnny to learn from his mistakes than simply to suffer immediate consequences. Learning from consequences may actually be more important than learning about them.

Plans, Schematics, and Building Codes

From Drawings to Schematics:
The Road To Hell Is Paved With Good Intentions

Tyrell created a common purpose with Johnny through their little discussion. But a common purpose alone does not create desired results. Csikszentmihalyi (1990) tells us that if we want our children to develop a sense of efficacy, what he calls flow, they must first understand the goal, then believe they have the skills to achieve it, and finally receive adequate feedback to know how close they are coming to the target. The purpose of architectural drawings is to try out different design ideas to determine what they could look like on paper. *"I thought I wanted a winding staircase until I realized how much space it would take from a house and how expensive it can be."* Drawings create an ambiance, a feeling. But it takes schematic drawings to bring the costs of those feelings to reality.

Hiring an architect to design your home is both time-consuming and expensive. It is definitely less trouble up front to follow a ready made set of plans. Likewise, being an architect can be exasperating. People say they want a particular feel, but often they don't know what that really means and they are seldom willing to pay for it in time or money. "I wanted to be different, but not that different."

Tyrell and Johnny created drawings for Johnny's Color home from their original conversation. But they had only begun the building process. Contractors cannot use architectural drawings alone to build a house. They need engineering schematics to paint the entire picture. How many outlets do you want in your house? That depends on what appliances you plan to have. But if you don't have adequate power, you will limit your

Plans, Schematics, and Building Codes

appliance options for the future. How high should your windows be, and what dimensions should they have? Will you have double pane windows, brick, or aluminum siding, one story or two...?

Parents need to help their children paint a picture of success. What could my ideal Color home look like, and what will it cost me to build it? And gee whiz, I didn't realize how much it would cost me to maintain it.

Deciding how many rooms a home should have, whether or not you want a formal dining room, or how large the bedrooms should be are all matters of architectural design. However, architectural drawings are not complete without a set of schematics for wiring, plumbing, and heating. These are the support structures for your home, the systems that make it work. As you help your children design their Color home, you need to engineer ways for them to live and grow in it. Things like the heating system, a central vacuum, electrical outlets, and telecommunications wiring enrich your child's home making it a safe and pleasant place to live. What do the schematics for your children's Color home look like?

One way to think of schematics for child rearing is to consider the kinds of supporting structures your child needs to develop a healthy life style. In his book, *Building The Bridge As You Walk On It* (2004) Robert Quinn speaks of eight characteristics that allow people to take charge of their lives: reflective action, authentic engagement, appreciative inquiry, grounded vision, adaptive confidence, detached interdependence, responsible freedom, and tough love. Although Quinn's book focuses on leadership, these eight characteristics provide a great way for parents to develop schematics for child rearing. Let's consider these eight characteristics individually in terms of your child's Color rainbow.

Reflective action involves thinking about our actions before, during, and after an event. It is a great way for a human architect to model all eight characteristics. Figure 3.1 illustrates how you can build on reflective action to model the kinds of attitudes and behaviors you want your children to develop.

A Reflective Action Rainbow
Figure 3.1

Color	Reflection	Action
Blue	On people and relationships	When personal relationships are involved
Gold	On rules and values	When situations are predictable
Green	On ideas and principles	When principles are aligned
Orange	On how I can channel my energy	When thrill or challenge is involved

Reflection is primarily a Green function. But as we will consider in more detail in the next chapter, if we want to teach children a skill, we need to play to their strengths.

Roberto's primary Color is Blue. He reflects a great deal about people and he is most likely to act when personal relationships are involved. Julio,

Plans, Schematics, and Building Codes

Roberto's dad, is an Orange, and he wants Roberto to play sports. Even though Roberto appears to be a natural at many sports, he is not as competitive as many of his friends. In baseball Roberto seems satisfied to be a part of the team and to play a few innings each week. But now that Roberto is 13 and in pony league, Julio has noticed that some of his friends are not paying as much attention to Roberto. He senses that Roberto is a bit depressed about this, and he wants to help.

Plans, Schematics, and Building Codes

Roberto and the Baseball Friendship

"I notice that you and Bruce don't hang as much together lately, Roberto. What's going on?"

"Oh, he's gotten really good at baseball, and he likes to hang with Joey and the other starters."

"So, is Bruce's friendship important to you?"

"Oh yeah, but it's not as important to Bruce. But that's okay."

"Roberto, Bruce loves baseball. He eats, sleeps, and dreams baseball. Part of friendship is having something in common. What could you do to strengthen your relationship with Bruce?"

"Do you mean I should practice being nicer to Bruce?" asked Roberto.

"Well, we should always think of ways to be nice to friends. But what makes people like someone else?"

"Well, I like people who are nice to me and my friends."

"Right, but how are people nice to your friends?"

"By showing interest in the things my friends like to do… But I am interested in baseball. I'm just more interested in my friends."

"How could you show Bruce that you are interested in him?"

"Oh, I get it. I could show more interest by practicing to get better and help the team win more games."

"That's a good idea. You see, winning isn't everything. But Bruce works hard at baseball, and winning is his payoff. You don't have to work at baseball as hard as Bruce works, but could you work a little bit harder than you have been? Perhaps you and I could practice your game more so that you have more in common with Bruce and the other guys. After all, as a friend you want to do as much as you can to help the team, don't you?"

"Yeah, I guess I could practice more. Would you really be willing to work with me, dad?"

1. Reflective Action

Did you notice how Julio talked with Roberto? He focused on Roberto's strength – friendships. Did you notice how he focused the goal on Roberto's friendship with Bruce, pointing out how practicing his game might give them more in common? How might this conversation have differed if Roberto's primary Color had been Gold? Go back to the chart and think about where Julio might have focused their reflective conversation. Your role as a human architect is to develop schematics that work for your children. Focus on their strengths.

For a Gold, reflective conversations might focus on the values of being a "contributing" member of the team. The other players may not expect you to get a hit every time you come to the plate, but they want you to give your best. We know the fundamentals. Now lets practice this game."

For a Green reflective conversations might focus on analyzing what you are doing well and where one or two simple improvements might enhance your game. "*You know, I've been watching you play, and I think your strengths are your bat and your arm. In the field, you seem to be slow finding the ball when it comes off the bat. I could show you a couple of films on how major league outfielders learn to anticipate where the ball is likely to go based on the pitch that has been thrown and the sound of the bat.*"

This Green conversation might also work with an Orange as long as the focus moved quickly to practice, engagement. "*You know, I've been watching you play, and I think your strengths are your bat and your arm. In the field, you seem to be slow finding the ball when it comes off the bat. I could*

*show you a couple of films on how major league outfielders learn to antic-
ipate where the ball is likely to go based on the pitch that has been thrown
and the sound of the bat. We'll take a look at the film tonight, and then
we'll hit the field this week and work on it."*

Notice that in each situation the parent architect is...

- *Building a common commitment with the child.*
- *Providing equal access to pertinent information.*
- *Collaborating and reflecting in terms of something the child
  loves to do and for which he has some skill.*
- *Leading and facilitating the planning but focusing on the
  child's needs.*

Let's use this same conversation to determine whether or not Julio has
engaged with Roberto authentically.

2. Authentic Engagement

Authentic engagement involves having a purpose higher than yourself,
setting your ego aside and showing a true love for what you are doing. He
got into the joy of the moment as he helped Roberto reflect on who he
was and what was important to him. He also sent the message that he was
willing to help. As a human architect, you need to offer your help willingly
and enthusiastically rather than sounding as if you feel obligated.

Julio set his ego aside. His purpose was obviously higher than simply
making Roberto a better ball player than his friends. Their practice together

will not only make Roberto a better ball player. If Julio makes this a positive experience, he and Roberto will build a closer bond. Julio's joy will come through that interaction and through watching Roberto learn how to work on his own problem solutions.

3. Appreciative Inquiry

Appreciative inquiry involves not telling your children what to do or manipulating them to "see things your way." Julio asked Roberto positive questions based on Roberto's way of looking at the world. As a human architect, you cannot approach your children's problems through your primary Color. You accept their Color by entering the inquiry through it.

As an Orange parent you may need to suspend your own sense of competition. As a Gold parent you may need to suspend your tendency to judge or "correct." As a Green parent you may need to suspend your tendency toward analysis paralysis. As a Blue you may need to look beyond your tendency to seek comfort and avoid controversy.

4. Grounded Vision

Again, as a parent you are the architect advising the homeowner. This is your child's home. The vision of what the home should look like belongs to the child. It should be grounded in the child's strengths and supported by the parents' strengths. Notice that Julio talked to Roberto about why baseball was important to him. It was about friendships. He asked Roberto why baseball was important to him, knowing that first and foremost Roberto saw baseball as an opportunity to interact with his friends.

You probably want your children to be happy productive citizens, to feel a sense of purpose in their life. Children do not have the advantage of life experiences, but even at a very young age they have a sense of purpose. They feel very deeply about things, and therein lies the key. Julio focused his discussion with Roberto on what he saw as important. He encouraged Roberto to look at his priorities and to consider how his actions might be impacting those priorities. What do you want, and how are you acting on your goals? Often children can be very clear on their goals, but they may lack the ability to articulate them. That is why appreciative inquiry, questioning that guides your children's thinking, is so important. Julio used his questions to trigger Roberto's reflective action, to help him develop a vision.

5. Adaptive Confidence

It is important to help your children develop a sense of self-confidence. However, it is not a good idea to develop self-confidence at the expense of another person. Julio focused on Roberto's friendships and reminded him that he had athletic skills. He did not chide him for failing to practice. He did not tell him that he was better than the other boys or even suggest that competition was an appropriate goal in this situation. Julio recognized that Bruce "lived for baseball." He also recognized that Roberto played the game to be with his friends. Julio knew that Roberto could improve his friendships with Bruce and the other players if he simply improved his game a notch or two – becoming a teammate they could count on when he was playing.

Everyone has certain talents. It is not necessary for your child to be good at everything. But being good enough at some things can be very important in their lives. Sports are often one of those things, particularly for boys (and today it is often equally important for girls). Regardless of the skill or activity, you can remind your children to use the Four-P's to analyze their options.

Purpose	Why is this skill or activity important to me?
Parameter	What are my abilities and interests related to this skill or activity?
Principles	How can I improve my skills in this area?
Priorities	Am I willing to work at this activity, or should I redirect my efforts?

To develop adaptive confidence, children need to think about their options. Do they have the skills necessary to compete in a particular area? If not, are they willing to work on those skills? Adaptive confidence involves more than the skills necessary to compete. It involves knowing why something is important as well as knowing its relative importance to other activities. If Roberto did not like baseball at all, Julio might have needed to help him consider other activities where he could pursue his friendship with Bruce and the other players. What other options might you have considered in this situation?

6. Detached Interdependence

As human beings we are dependent on other people for feedback and support. Remember the Colors adage, *"Be your Color, but learn to do all of the Colors."* This adage summarizes detached interdependence. Julio did not encourage Roberto to be like Bruce and the other players. He encouraged Roberto to think about what was important to him (Bruce and the other players' friendship) and then to do what he needed to do to achieve his purpose. Julio was helping Roberto to think about what was important to him – helping Roberto to detach from his friends and from the game of baseball long enough to think about his own purpose. Roberto liked being with his friends.

Like Julio, you can help your children detach from the moment to consider their purpose. Help them separate their goals from other peoples' goals and to see beyond a particular activity or event to their underlying concerns. But often parents try to help their children by saying such things as, *"Oh well, I have always thought Bruce was self-centered anyhow;"* or *"You don't need friends like that."* Part of developing healthy relationships with others is recognizing how your own happiness and well-being can gather strength from and contribute strength to someone else – interdependence.

7. *Responsible Freedom*

A key line in the song, *Me and Bobby McGee* (1968) says, *"Freedom's just another word for nothing left to lose."* You can help your children understand that complete freedom is very costly, if not impossible, to achieve in this world. We are as dependent on others as they are on us – interdependence. You can teach your children that they can be free to follow their own dreams without ignoring their responsibilities. This is the Eastern philosophy of "doing no harm."

Let's return to Julio's discussion with Roberto for a moment.

> *"So, is Bruce's friendship important to you?"*

> *"Oh yeah, but not as important to Bruce. But that's okay."*

> *"Roberto, Bruce loves baseball. He eats, sleeps, and dreams baseball. Part of friendship is having something in common. Perhaps you and I could practice your game more so that you had more in common with Bruce and the other guys. After all, as a friend you want to do as much as you can to help the team, don't you?"*

> *"Yeah, I guess I could practice more. Would you really be willing to work with me, dad?"*

Julio used this opportunity to model responsible freedom with Roberto. Your children can learn to pursue their own goals in ways that do not interfere with other people's goals. In fact, you can teach your children that helping other people achieve their goals is often the easier way to achieve their own goals – responsible freedom. (I get what I want and you get what you want.) Children need to learn how to help friends achieve their goals without assuming responsibility for their friends' happiness.

8. Tough Love

Parents sometimes confuse tough love with being stern. *"If I love my children, I must be demanding."* In reality, the tough part of tough love has more to do with parents being tough on themselves. Tough love requires you to take the extra time necessary to help your children solve their own problems rather than waiting for you to tell them what to do. It is often tough for parents to give their children opportunities to fail. It takes extra time and planning to create safe opportunities for children to learn from their mistakes.

When Julio offered to spend time practicing baseball with Roberto, he realized that Roberto was probably not going to become a regular starter on the team. He also realized that he would need to spend his time working with Roberto to improve his skills to an acceptable level. But Julio saw this as an opportunity to spend time with Roberto and to show Roberto that friendships could be worth working for. It would have been far easier initially for Julio to have encouraged Roberto to find new friends. But this would have sent several messages that Julio wanted to avoid: that friends come and go, that it is less painful to walk away than to work for what you want, that there is not much you can do when life deals you a bad hand.

Julio used the eight human architectural characteristics to help Roberto build his own Color home. Think about how you can help your children design a home for their own personality. At the same time, don't forget that your children need to understand that every community has its own unique set of building codes. Let's consider for a moment how those codes can affect your children's Color decisions.

Negotiating Local Building Codes

How many times have you said something like this? *"I don't care what anybody thinks; I'm going to live my life the way I want to live it."* To live our own dreams is a very positive life choice. To do so without considering the consequences is short sighted and naive.

Every group, family, or community has its own mores or ways of doing things. Sometimes these customs are clearly stated, but often they are very subtle.

- *We don't raise our voices in this house.*
- *God gave you two ears and one mouth for a reason.*
- *We respect our elders.*
- *Children are to be seen and not heard.*

As you think about some of these beliefs or customs, ask yourself the following questions:

- *Do I think boys should be tough and competitive?*
- *Do I prefer girls to be shy and compliant?*
- *Do I expect boys to play with cars and trucks and girls to play with dolls and tea sets?*
- *Do I think of men as the breadwinners and women as the homemakers?*
- *Do I put work before family?*
- *Do I categorize people – good or bad; smart or slow; motivated or lazy; etc.?*
- *Do I...*

Intentionally or unintentionally, most of us make judgments about other people. Even when we try to be less judgmental, our actions often speak louder than our words. As a parent, you need to recognize your own prejudices and learn to monitor how closely your words match your actions. Honesty is walking your talk; whereas, integrity is talking your walk. Simply stated, it is better to admit your prejudices to your children and to encourage your children to avoid them than to pretend that you have no prejudices at all. Children learn more from our actions than from our words. And if our words and actions are not consistent, our children can develop double standards at a very early age.

As a human architect, you have a tremendous impact on your children's Color home. Make certain that you live up to your responsibilities. Don't forget whose home you are designing. Don't use them to live your Color dreams. Don't design their home for your "stuff." Be honest with them about both the strengths and challenges their preferred design entails. Help them understand the building codes that exist within your family, your neighborhood, and the community as a whole. Being an effective human architect requires both you and your children to be open and honest with one another. It requires patience and communication. Most of all, it requires you as the architect to practice the eight skills discussed in this chapter until they become a personal habit for you and a positive model for your children.

To lead is to guide, especially by going in advance (Webster, 1991). You cannot tell your children how to create their Color home, but you can give them sound architectural advice. Parenting is a life long commitment. It can become a life long joy as well if you learn to focus on success. But before we move to this next level of effective parenting habits, take a moment to consider the items on the next couple of pages.

Developing Plans, Schematics, and Building Codes

1. What decisions are my children ready to make on their own, and what support/guidance will they need from me? (Consider age, maturity, and experiences.)

2. Do I have the necessary skills and information to provide this support? (Think of your Color rainbow as opposed to your children's Color rainbows.)

Color	My Order (1-4)	My Child's Order (1-4)
Blue		
Gold		
Green		
Orange		

Plans, Schematics, and Building Codes

3. Where are my Color preferences likely to collide with my children's preferences?

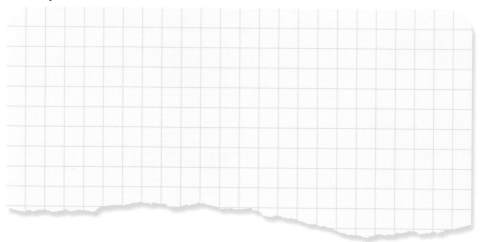

4. Whom will you rely on to assist you with your architectural work? (Consider how well you can make plans and design schematics, as well as how well you can read community customs and mores.)

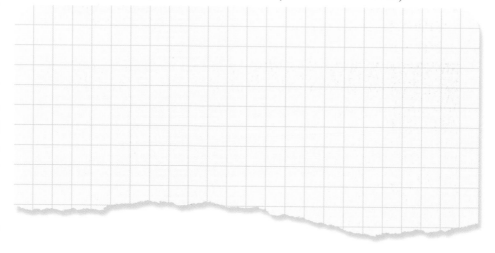

Plans, Schematics, and Building Codes

5. What is your comfort with each of the eight human architectural habits and what is your timeline for developing them?

Reflective action

Authentic engagement

Appreciative inquiry

Grounded vision

Adaptive confidence

Detached interdependence

Responsible freedom

Tough love

Plans, Schematics, and Building Codes

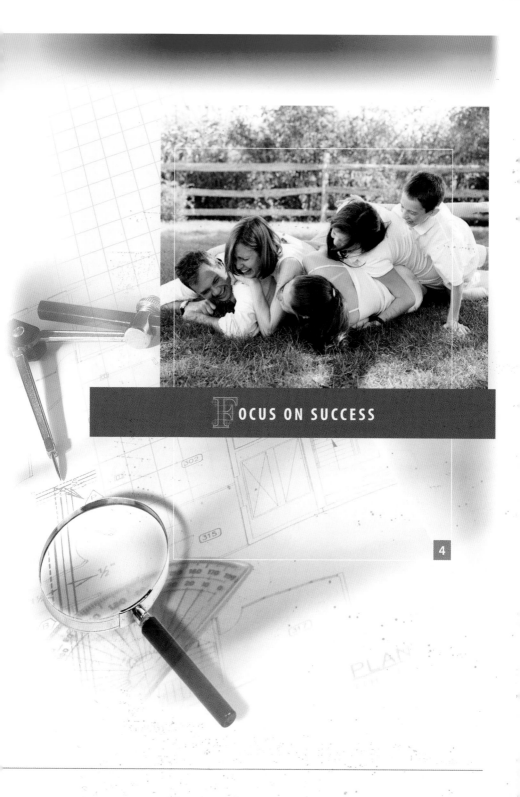

FOCUS ON SUCCESS

4

Joy is a Green-Orange adolescent. Throughout her elementary school years she was a star student and every teacher's favorite child. She was academically bright, articulate, and simply a wonderful addition to any situation. Joy was naturally polite and mature but seemed to work at being perfect. Her father and mother showered praise on her and seldom needed to deal with inappropriate behaviors.

But when Joy reached middle school, she went through an amazing transformation. Her grades dropped precipitously, she started "hanging" with the "wrong crowd" of friends, and she became anything but the teachers' favorite student. Now thirteen, Joy's latest problems included being caught in a raid of a high school party where alcohol, marijuana, and sex were available.

Joy's parents were beside themselves. Her Blue-Gold mother, Frances, was mortified to think that she had "failed so miserably as a parent." Her Orange-Blue father, Ted, felt betrayed by the "little girl" who had always been the center of his world. During family counseling, the psychologist asked Joy what she thought had led to this drastic change in her life.

"I don't really know for sure," Joy responded. "I know I've disappointed my mom and dad. I've disappointed myself too."

"It's not about us," Frances sobbed. "You're father and I just want you to be happy."

"I want my little girl back," Ted stuttered.

"But dad, I'm not your little girl anymore. I'm thirteen years old. I love Jake and would have proven it to him at the party if the police hadn't raided us. I'm tired of being what everyone else expects. That "good girl" stuff is okay for elementary kids, but it doesn't work in middle school. Most boys don't like smart girls, and those who do are geeks. To be one of the in-crowd, I'd have to act like an elementary kid. Most of my classmates are so immature that they bore me. I know that isn't kind to say, but it's true."

Focus on Success

"Lately you and mom do nothing but tell me how much you loved me when I did everything your way. You guys don't realize that I didn't quit learning just because my grades went south. Jake and I love to read poetry. We even read Shakespeare together. You didn't seem to mind me being with Jake when he was my tutor, when he was helping me improve my grades so I could be your good little girl again. He and I work on his geometry and chemistry projects together, and he is teaching me to write short stories. Smart doesn't mean just getting good grades. You guys always told me that in elementary school. 'Follow your dreams,' you told me. Well Jake is one of my dreams. Were all those things you told me just hollow words? Does anyone really care who I want to be? I know I embarrassed you in front of your church friends, Mom. And Dad, you can't brag about me to the guys at work anymore. But is that all I am – your toy? I'm a person, a smart, loving person. And I'm tired of being the cute little smart girl."

Joy is a classic case of a Green-Orange girl whose architect parents forgot to check the local building codes when she moved into adolescence. If they had, they might have realized that what adults see as positive characteristics in a child are not necessarily the same characteristics that make that child popular with friends. The stereotype for girls in our society is still that they should be soft and caring – intelligent, but not too intelligent. Adolescent boys still tend to seek the macho role and expect girls not to challenge that position. The maturity that makes girls popular during their elementary years often makes them feel out of place at the middle school level. They sometimes find the normal middle school friends and activities to be beneath them. In this situation they often seek the company of older friends for whom their intelligence and maturity poses less of a threat. Unfortunately, as in Joy's situation, those relationships sometimes lead them into situations that they are not socially or psychologically prepared for.

But you might ask, *"I thought this chapter was about focusing on success. And Joy's parents certainly focused on her success throughout her preadolescent years. Where did they go wrong?"*

Parenting mistakes do not always involve selfishness or neglect. In fact, they are often more about missing the signs, being unaware of the local building codes. Frances and Ted had failed to see that the building codes for a middle school child change from those of an elementary school child. Parents and teachers like bright girls and sensitive boys. But those characteristics are not necessarily at the top of the building code list for adolescents. In early adolescence, boys and girls alike are trying to find their own identity. Unfortunately, they often turn to their friends for cues since they are spending many more of their waking hours with friends: school, after school activities, sleepovers, etc. As several recent ad campaigns are stressing, however, adolescents still rely on their parents' opinions. Unfortunately, parents often fail to recognize that while the purpose of their children's lives may not have changed, the parameters have. Let's consider for a moment how the reflective action rainbow evolves over time.

Focusing On Success: An Evolutionary Process

Figure 4.1 provides an evolutionary view of a reflective action rainbow. Notice how the building codes (positive expectations) change slightly as a child grows. Notice also that they do not have exactly the same impact on children of differing Color preferences. The first three columns of this chart are the same as Figure 3.1 on page 80. The next two columns, however, demonstrate the shifting nature of building codes as children enter adolescence. In many cases these changes are gradual and can be dealt with through routine support mechanisms between parents and other caregivers. In some situations the changes seem to occur overnight. They are anything but subtle, and they can pose significant risks for kids as well as for their families. As you review this chart, think about how your children's Color rainbow might affect their change process and how your Color rainbow might affect your reactions to that change.

Remember, reflection is primarily a Green function. Ironically, those adolescents who reflect on parents' spoken words versus their actions often find a disconnect between the two. And those who reflect logically on their peers' words and actions often find themselves criticized and excluded from the group. Boys often act out in what appears to be less mature behavior to win an approving laugh from friends. Girls, who tend to mature more quickly than boys in many cases, often act out in what appear to be more adult-like behaviors: disdainful sighs, rolling eyes, and smiles that say, "Adults simply don't get it."

An Evolving Reflective Action Rainbow
Figure 4.1

Color	Reflection	Action	Childhood Building Codes	Adolescent Building Codes
Blue	On people and relationships	When personal relationships are involved	Personal relationships influenced more by adults	Adult influence competes with peer influence on a more regular basis
Gold	On rules and values	When situations are predictable	Adult rules and values guide children's decisions	Adult rules and values compete with other families' rules and values in less predictable situations
Green	On ideas and principles	When principles are aligned	Most opportunities to test ideas and principles are tested with adults	More opportunities arise where ideas and principles can be compared among adolescents and in other homes
Orange	On how I can improve	When thrill or challenge is involved	Adults have much closer supervision of the level and intent of challenge and risk	More opportunities arise to test limits and challenge the status quo

Figure 4.1 illustrates how children not only face changing adult expectations as they enter adolescence. They face changing expectations from peers and from older friends and siblings. Where earlier they had simply trusted adult

admonitions, they now realize that the building codes established in their homes are not universally accepted. *"Other kids' parents don't make them..."*

What these emerging adolescents need from parents and other adult care-givers is more frequent opportunities to test their adolescent hypotheses about life. At this point in their lives it is important for parent architects to balance their sense of concern with an openness to their children's points-of-view. But how do Blue parents know when they are being too accommodating of their children's "inappropriate" behaviors? How do Gold parents know when they are being too judgmental? How do Green parents know when they are being too indirect or over-analyzing? How do Orange parents know when they are being too nonchalant about risky adolescent behaviors? Again, Quinn's *Eight Characteristics of Leadership* (2004) provide a useful guide through changing adolescent building codes.

 Joy's primary Color is Green. She reflects a great deal about ideas and principles, and she is most likely to act or speak out when those principles are being violated. Since most adolescents are concerned about fitting in with their peers, Joy's need to analyze people's actions according to certain principles may not sit well with Gold girls who expect their friends to "stick together." It may not sit well with Orange boys who are focused on

having a good time and impressing friends rather than following some abstract principle about basic human responsibilities. Blue friends may find Joy's analyses and tendencies to be direct as an affront to good manners.

Joy's mother is Blue-Gold. She wants peace and predictability. Her father is Orange-Blue. He appreciates Joy's outspoken intelligence, but he has been unpleasantly surprised with the direction in which it has taken her and the strain it has placed on their relationship.

1. Reflective Action

Given Joy's candid statements during her counseling session, how might Frances and Ted engage with her in a reflective action process that focuses on Joy's strengths? First, they can honor Joy's honesty. They can also recognize her continued interest in learning. Although they probably do not want her dating a sixteen-year-old boy, they need to consider the nature of teen-age relationships. They tend more often to be short-term when they are not totally opposed by parents. *"You have always said that I am more mature than the kids my age, and you have always told me to hang around with kids who share my values. How then can you tell me not to love Jake?"*

Obviously Frances and Ted have a dilemma. Joy has indicated that she has intended several high risk behaviors as a part of her relationship with a high school student. Rather than forbidding Joy to see Jake, Frances and Ted focus their attention on Joy's inappropriate behaviors.

"*So do you have any suggestions about an appropriate consequence for your actions?*" *asks Ted.*

"*I know I should be grounded. But this is the first time I've used drugs or alcohol. I did lie to you and Mom about where I was going.*"

"*I think we need to continue counseling for a while too,*" *adds Frances.* "*We seem to need some help with communication. This is the most you have shared with your father and me for some time. And Joy, this was a serious mistake and a significant breach of your father's trust, and mine. How long do you think your grounding should last?*"

"*I guess maybe three or four months,*" *whispers Joy.*

"*Well, I think perhaps we should take this in steps. You will be grounded for the next six weeks. Then if we see your grades and behavior improving at school, we will consider allowing kids to come to our house one night on the weekend for the following six weeks. And that even includes Jake, if he wants to come.*"

"*Really? Jake?*"

"*Your father and I are not going to tell you that you cannot see Jake. But you are too young to date, and you have both indicated that you are less mature than even you had thought. Your behav-*

*iors were a betrayal of our trust and a foolish example of irre-
sponsibility. You will both need to earn my trust again. But you
and Jake have common interests. If your father and I are willing
to accept that you are more mature than some of the kids your
age, you and Jake need to accept that you are still too young to
date and obviously not yet able to deal with the temptations of
the high school world. "*

Parents often exact consequences that are difficult to manage. If Frances
and Ted had accepted Joy's three or four month self-imposed grounding
sentence, one of them would have needed to stay home to monitor Joy
during that entire period. They knew they were taking a risk in allowing
Joy's romance with Jake to continue in any form, but they had to weigh that
against the effects of turning this young couple into Romeo and Juliet. By
insisting on a continuation of the family counseling, Frances also indicated
that she and Ted were willing to work on their communications with Joy.
Frances refused to accept responsibility for Joy's mistakes, but she demonstrated unconditional love and support.

As Julio did in the last chapter, Frances was...

- *Building a common commitment with Joy.*

- *Providing equal access to pertinent information.*

- *Collaborating and reflecting in terms of something Joy loves
  without placing her into another high-risk situation.*

- *Leading and facilitating the planning but focusing on Joy's needs.*

2. Authentic Engagement

Frances obviously focused on a purpose higher than herself. She took a risk in allowing Joy to continue seeing Jake. But she insisted that Joy prove herself before Jake would be permitted to visit their home. By continuing the family counseling, Frances was also encouraging Joy to focus on something higher than herself, winning back her parents' trust.

It was not easy for the Blue-Gold Frances to set aside her pain and fear. However, she recognized that Joy was more likely to turn her life around if she had to live with her own mistakes rather than being allowed to turn her anger into martyrdom. And Frances was also not ashamed to admit that she and Ted needed help in communicating with their adolescent daughter. Joy's needs superceded Frances' ego.

3. Appreciative Inquiry

Did you notice that Frances' appreciative inquiry led Joy toward a higher level of self-analysis and trust? Frances alluded to her Blue sense of betrayal and to Joy's breaking Frances' sense of appropriate Gold parameters. Yet she focused on logic. She described Joy's mistakes in logical, unemotional terms. Frances communicated a belief in Joy's ability to regain her trust. She made the consequence timelines reasonable and established a clear target for Joy to prove herself.

As an Orange parent, Ted held back in this discussion. He recognized that he might allow his disappointment to drive unrealistic expectations or to encourage a match of wills with Joy. Frances identified Joy's unacceptable behavior, but she did not focus on her "still being a child." She recognized Joy's immaturity "in this situation" but challenged her to live up to a level of which she was certainly capable.

4. Grounded Vision

This was a situation where Joy was seeking more mature friends. Her choices simply indicated a dangerous lack of experience. Joy felt like a happy, productive individual. She and Jake read poetry, studied geometry and chemistry together, and wrote short stories. They shared the same values. By establishing a way for Jake and Joy to continue a limited and monitored relationship, Frances and Ted were placing the responsibility squarely at their feet – prove that you can be mature enough to recognize our concerns as parents.

Adolescents love as much as they know how at any given moment. But it is typically not healthy to allow younger teenage girls to date older teenage boys. Frances did not deny or belittle Joy's feelings for Jake. She simply established reasonable limitations under which they would operate. "I recognize that you have to find your own way in life eventually, but do you recognize how you acted on your goals?" The need for appreciative inquiry doesn't stop when kids move from childhood to adolescence. It simply changes forms.

5. Adaptive Confidence

Frances had helped Joy develop a sense of self-confidence. However, that very strength took on a negative bent when Joy entered the realm of love – her first real love. Joy had handled herself effectively throughout grade school. Frances and Ted had not manipulated or coerced her into becoming a high achieving child, and they should not allow her to manipulate them now into accepting blame for her mistakes. Joy's sense of Green logic worked effectively for her throughout childhood. But love and acceptance are not necessarily based on logic and achievement.

Frances knew that if she was going to build on Joy's success, she needed to help her adapt to the changing world of adolescence. She wanted Joy to see that she could have both high achievement and positive relationships. And she also recognized that given time, Joy's classmates would become more mature and more interested in achieving in school. She needed to help Joy navigate her way through this new mine field of challenges, to gain a new sense of confidence in various new situations.

Like younger children, adolescents need to think about their options. Adaptive confidence involves more than adapting skills. It involves sorting through emotions to find a deeper meaning, a deeper sense of purpose. Would you have allowed your thirteen-year-old daughter to continue seeing a sixteen-year-old boy even on the limited terms that Frances and Ted established? If not, what other options might you have considered in this situation?

6. Detached Interdependence

Detached interdependence requires adolescents to look beyond the people they love to consider the course of their own lives. Frances did not forbid Joy to see Jake. She quietly hoped they might grow apart during Joy's initial six weeks of being grounded. She also quietly hoped that seeing Joy one evening on the weekend in her home might encourage Jake to find someone his own age to date. At the same time, Frances recognized that for the next six weeks she was going to control the nature of this adolescent relationship. At the very least, she and Ted had bought time – time for Joy to improve her grades and renew her interest in school achievement, time for them to learn more about the kind of boy Jake was, and time for Frances and Ted to consider ways to monitor Joy's relationship with Jake if it survived this twelve week period.

In this case, Frances and Ted were helping Joy to refocus on her own life, on what was important to her beyond Jake. Parent architects can help their children detach from the moment to consider their purpose. Adolescents need to learn that they do not need to abandon what is good for them in order to have friends or to experience loving relationships. Jake was not the problem here. Joy's grades and behavior had been deteriorating long before she met Jake. Joy had come to value approval from others more than her own sense of self-worth. Frances and Ted hoped they could encourage her to detach her purpose from approval – theirs or that of her friends. Again, part of developing healthy relationships with others evolves from recognizing how your own happiness and well-being can gather strength from and contribute strength to someone else – interdependence.

7. *Responsible Freedom*

Joy had not demonstrated responsible freedom. She had ignored her own well-being and had ignored her relationship with her parents. Frances and Ted wanted to show Joy that they trusted her to be free to follow her heart without abandoning her brains.

Frances guided Joy toward responsible freedom. She would allow Jake and Joy to be together in her home once each weekend when Joy showed that she could take responsibility for her own needs – doing well in school. Instead of building a wall to protect Joy from Jake, Frances challenged Joy to demonstrate responsibility in order to earn the freedom to have a boy-girl relationship appropriate to her age and level of maturity.

8. *Tough Love*

Here again Frances showed tough love not by being strict with Joy but by placing the responsibility in her lap. She accepted a share of the responsibility for communication, but she did not accept responsibility for Joy's mistakes. Frances took a risk in allowing Joy to continue her relationship with Jake. She allowed her a reasonable opportunity to fail within a safe environment.

Frances and Ted were willing to devote time both to monitoring Joy's activities for the next three months and to participating in family counseling sessions. They saw an opportunity to rebuild their relationship with Joy and to rebuild Joy's confidence in herself. Frances and Ted could have forbidden

Focus on Success

Joy to see Jake. They could have controlled her every movement for the three or four months of being grounded that Joy had herself recommended. But that would not have allowed Joy to bring her strengths back to the surface, to relearn what she already knew about herself.

Children do not learn from having parents control their behavior. They learn from opportunities to analyze the consequences of their own actions and from relying on their own strengths to rebuild their lives following difficult experiences. As parents you need to demonstrate your confidence in your children to solve their own problems. Talk to them about their strengths. Remind them to think about times when their lives brought them a deeper sense of joy rather than intermittent thrills surrounded by pain and disappointments. Your children will learn to cope with pain and mistakes when they know what is expected in a given situation, believe that they have the skills to meet those expectations, and learn how to monitor their own feedback with your love and support.

Levine (2002) encourages parents and other adult care-givers to shift their thinking to building on children's strengths. He cites examples from his 30 years of research and practice as a pediatrician of kids who have come to believe that success is being like other kids instead of celebrating their unique way of thinking. Levine cites examples of how adult expectations help to create student social groups: popular students, controversial students, amiable students, neglected students, and rejected students.

Focus on Success

Changing Attitudes

You don't stay awake at night conjuring up ways to make your children's lives miserable. In fact, you probably think you are doing the right thing when you show them how to do things "better." After all, you want them to be successful – right? And if they don't learn to be more_____... (You can fill in the blank with whatever skill you consider to be lacking.) ...they certainly won't be successful at...

Julio, Frances, and Ted are all examples of how even the most attentive and supportive parents can sometimes lose touch with their children. When most parents think about changing attitudes, they think about how to change their children's attitudes. They talk with other parents who have experienced similar difficulties or with parents whose children seem to have few major difficulties. Then they come to the conclusion that "if only we had..."

It is fine to discuss parenting with other parents, but you need to be careful about jumping to conclusions regarding changes that you need to make. "Group-think" can be as detrimental to parenting as can declaring open warfare with your children. Human architecture requires you to know and understand your children as individuals. It also requires you to know your own skill set – your strengths and liabilities. The litmus test for successful parenting is the extent to which your actions promote positive growth for both you and your children. If you don't see yourself as a learner in this relationship, you will not be a successful teacher.

Responsibilities within a parent-child relationship don't simply present themselves. Parenting is about modeling an ongoing willingness to learn and to grow with your children. You cannot change your children's personalities, but you can help them change their attitudes. Most people want to be around people who think and act the way they do. And because these are your children, you expect them to think and act in a manner consistent with your words and actions. Unfortunately, children often learn more from what their parents do than from what they say. As parents, we create a set of cultural expectations within our family. Those who significantly violate that culture simply do not understand the "way we do things around here."

All families develop a sense of "the way we do things." Imagine how difficult daily life would be if you had to analyze or second guess every experience. Too many surprises make family life difficult to manage. But too much probability can also pose a problem. As a parent architect you can help your family find a balance between boredom and chaos by approaching your differences as strengths rather than problems.

Figure 4.2 is an adaptation of a concept that I developed for my book, *Sustaining Change in Schools* (2005). It illustrates a hierarchy of skills that you can use within your family to improve your attitudes toward individual and group differences. Column one, based on Paul and Elder's *Concepts of Critical Thinking* (2001), suggests that before you can change an attitude, you must take the time to think about where it came from and how accurate it is. Column two, based on Chrislip's *Guide to Collaboration* (2002), illustrates how your family can learn to "get along" despite your differences. Finally, column three, based on Hartzler and Henry's *Four Areas of Team Fitness* (1994), illustrates how you can change your attitudes about what it means to be a family.

From Related Individuals To Functioning Family
Figure 4.2

Analyzing Family Attitudes	Changing Family Attitudes	Functioning As A Family
1. Recognizing what we share beyond our DNA (purpose)	**A. Getting Started** 1. Talking about situations where we need one another's support 2. Deciding on a plan to support one another	1. Identify and prioritize family needs
2. Asking the tough questions about our attitudes		2. Clarify expectations for a family win-win
3. Identifying assumptions we make about one another	**B. Setting up for Success** 1. Identifying expectations of one another	3. Understand individual and family strengths and liabilities
4. Identifying each member's point of view	2. Choosing opportunities to practice together	4. Take responsibility for established family values, beliefs, and priorities
5. Talking about specific good times and bad times	3. Deciding what support looks like to each person 4. Clarifying individual responsibilities	
6. Identifying how strings of incidents demonstrate underlying attitudes	**C. Deciding what needs to be done** 1. Family meetings	
7. Dealing with inferences family members draw from behaviors	2. Sharing our plans with others who might help	
8. Considering implications and consequences of our existing relationships		

Focus on Success

Positive family relationships don't happen in a vacuum. They are built. You and your children can either argue about who created your problems or choose to recognize them and work together toward solutions. Problems are much more easily solved when family members can work from a sense of adaptive confidence. That is, I am confident that I have the skills to contribute to a solution without having to get everything I want. And you can't wait until your children become adolescents to build a functioning family.

One day four-year-old Hanna asked her father, Pierce, why she needed to go to bed at 7:00. "You and Mommy said I was a big girl now. You said that big girls don't suck their thumbs and that big girls get to do things that little girls don't get to do. Sally stays up until 8:00. Why can't I?"

What should Pierce tell Hanna? What might he have told Hanna that contributed to her current question? Where does Pierce go from here? Let's return to the first column of Figure 4.2 to consider Pierce and Hanna's situation. Pierce might consider...

- *What is the purpose of a 7:00 bedtime?*

- *What mixed messages might Hanna have gained from the solution to her thumb sucking?*

- *How do Hanna and Pierce's assumptions about being a "big girl" differ?*

- *How might Pierce and Hanna discuss the difficulties of being four-years-old?*

- *How will Pierce's handling of this situation affect the trust between him and Hanna?*

Hanna is four-years-old, but her question about her bedtime raises an ethical problem for Pierce. Notice how Pierce moves through column two of Figure 4.2 to deal with a different set of building codes emerging with this stage in Hanna's life.

Focus on Success

Big Girl Hanna and the Later Bedtime

"You know what? I think I do need to think again about how big you are. You have been going to bed at 7:00 for a long time now. And you did quit sucking your thumb. That does make you a big girl. You probably should be allowed to stay up later. Shouldn't you?"

"Really?"

"Well, yes. But we need to make a plan. Let's think for a moment. Mommy and my bedtime is usually 10:00. Sally's bedtime is 8:00. Right?"

"Yes."

"I'm really sorry that Mommy and I let you down on this one, Hanna. Now you aren't quite as big as Sally, and Sally isn't quite as big as Mommy and me. So let's think about what a new bedtime could be for a four-year-old big girl who quit sucking her thumb. Do you think you could stay up until 7:15 without being cranky the next day?"

"Sure."

"Well, let's try 7:15 starting tonight. But we need to have a plan. Fifteen minutes is a long time. How would we know if staying up until 7:15 was making you cranky?"

"If I was cranky, I would cry and argue with Sally, and…"

"Okay, let's bring Sally and Mommy in here and see if they would be willing to help us get you started on the right foot for this new 7:15 bedtime. You know, we all have to help one another if we want this new bedtime to work."

Finally, listen to the brief meeting Pierce and his family had as a means of working together to help Hanna. Notice how it follows column three in Figure 4.2.

"Sally, do you remember when you were having trouble doing your homework when Hanna was making noise upstairs?"

"Yes."

See how the story concludes on the next page!

*"And as you remember, we all talked about how Mommy and
I could play with Hanna downstairs until you finished your
homework, and then you agreed to play with Hanna for a few
minutes after you completed your homework."*

"Yes."

*"Well, as you know, Hanna has quit sucking her thumb now,
and that makes her a big girl – not as big as you, but pretty big.
So Mommy and I were thinking that maybe we could all help
Hanna have a new bedtime of 7:15 instead of 7:00. Do you think
you could help Mommy with the dogs so that I could read Hanna
her bedtime story at 7:00 instead of 6:45?"*

"Sure."

*"That is great. Your mother and I always appreciate how you
girls help one another out this way. That's what makes our
family work. Now, let's think for a minute about what other
responsibilities we may each need to assume since our schedule
will be changing."*

Blues require different assurances than do Golds, who require different
assurances than do Greens, who require different assurances than do
Oranges. Because of these Color differences within your family, you need to
develop a common purpose, and that purpose needs to address everyone's
strengths and liabilities. Think about how Sally might have felt if Pierce had

allowed Hanna to stay up as late as Sally. As a parent architect you need to remember how the various family members' building codes affect and are affected by agreements made between any two individuals. Building codes defining how big "big is" are important to family harmony. You need to think about the positive and negative affects of family decisions on each member of the family. With a bit of planning, you can celebrate differences and use them for every family member's benefit.

Effective family dialogue requires effective facilitation. Parents are the family architects. You have knowledge and skills that your children lack due to their level of experience and development. If you are satisfied simply to remind them that you know best, how will they develop the kinds of skills they will need to make decisions when you are not available to tell them what to do?

Jasmine, my secretary, recently asked me how she was supposed to find time to hold these family meetings. *"Raising children is not an easy task. By the time Lenny and I get home from work, we are both tired. Once we get dinner and help the kids with their homework, we are all too tired to have a family meeting. I just don't think parenting should become a chore. It seems to me that a little more common sense is what it takes to make parenting work."*

"That's fascinating," I replied. *"You didn't blink an eye when I asked you to take those technology classes to improve our Web page. Those classes took you more than a year to complete going two nights each week to class.*

Focus on Success

And just last week you told me you thought parenting was the most important responsibility any person can have. Do you mean to tell me you can find the time to learn technology skills for work, but you can't find the time to focus on 'the most important responsibility in your life?' Is there something wrong here?" I asked with a grin.

Family meetings don't need to be hard work. If you engage authentically with your children, these meetings can become a very positive experience. Through appreciative inquiry you can develop a grounded family vision that builds responsible freedom among all family members. Notice that Pierce did not ask Sally to be responsible for Hanna's new bedtime. He asked her if she would be willing to help Hanna achieve success with her new bedtime just as Hanna had helped Sally achieve success with her homework – detached interdependence.

Family meetings model reflective action. They help children understand how family guidelines contribute to every member's success. They help children set realistic goals, monitor their progress, and contribute to something greater than their own individual interests. These are all skills that apply well beyond childhood, well beyond adolescence. These are life-long skills. By modeling these skills with your children, you can develop positive attitudes about interacting with other people in multiple situations.

Have you noticed that the skills and strategies described in this chapter require attitudinal changes? And have you also noticed that since adult attitudes are often much more entrenched than are children's attitudes, they

Focus on Success

will probably be much more difficult to change. Tough love is tough. As a parent architect it can be difficult to lay aside your own attitudes and values in order to engage in appreciative inquiry. But you are not building your Color home. You are helping your children design their home.

You can structure family meetings to avoid issues of control or manipulation. Your children know who is in charge. In fact, they want to know that you will be there to make some decisions without a great deal of discussion. Obviously you do not have the time to hold a family meeting for every decision in your daily lives. But regular meetings, even if only held once each month, can bring families together for a common purpose.

Parents often ask their children, "Why didn't you come to me with this problem?" Don't wait for your children to come to you. They are young and lack experience. They may not even know the nature of a problem until it has grown too large for them to handle. Take the table to your children rather than waiting for them to come to you. It is not enough to have open communications in a family. Busy schedules and different definitions of what problems look like often get in the way of open communications. And don't underestimate how one negative experience inside or outside your family may negatively impact communications among family members. There is a fine line between being positive and being a Pollyanna. You can focus on success without ignoring problems. Hear the issues, identify the successes, and develop a plan.

Focus on Success

Not every family meeting will be a problem-solving situation. Sometimes they will serve only as a means of "touching base" with one another. But when you have used a family meeting to problem-solve, don't assume that you have captured the will and intent of family members without verifying your conclusions. Before closing a family meeting check for understanding. Take turns summarizing each other's responsibilities. Be certain to paint a clear picture of what success might look like. What would each family member be doing, seeing, and feeling if this situation goes according to plan?

Finally, don't ignore situations when one or more family members fail to live up to their responsibilities. Tough love is not as tough when you learn to confront small discrepancies before they become breeches of trust. Don't nitpick, but don't avoid holding one another accountable. Use these family meetings as opportunities to model life-long learning. Admit when you did not fulfill your family responsibilities, and demonstrate your willingness to correct your behavior. Remember, a positive attitude is far more significant in the long-term development of a trusting parent-child relationship than is a momentary failure to meet your responsibilities.

Summary

The story told by Mrs. Wallenda following the death of her husband who had fallen from a high wire offers some insight regarding the importance of focusing on success. When asked what her husband did differently on the day he fell to his death, Mrs. Wallenda responded, *"Instead of focusing on walking the wire, he was thinking about not falling."* The things that we choose to focus on have a tremendous impact on what we see. They have an equally significant impact on what our children learn to focus on.

Developing a shared purpose requires trust and understanding. It requires assurances that every family member has a place at the family table. As a parent architect you have a deeper understanding of the world than your children have. On the other hand, even the deepest understanding does not necessarily entitle parents to make every important decision. The question is not whether your children should listen to you, but how and when you should listen to them. To build an attitude of success, you must help your children look beyond authority and rules so that they can see the reasons underlying those parameters. You can help your children recognize that integrity is a matter of aligning their daily actions with their stated purpose. When you share information, you make it possible for your children to become responsible for success.

Before we turn to the fifth step involved with human architecture, let's take a moment to reflect on your parenting responsibilities. Do you and your family expect everyone to be responsible for success?

Focus on Success

1. In the graph below fill in your family members' Color rainbows by ranking each Color with 1 as the primary Color and 4 as the least relied on Color. (Add rows if you have more than two children.)

	Blue	Gold	Green	Orange
Me				
Spouse				
(Child's Name)				
(Child's Name)				

2. How does this mix of Color rainbows both enhance and challenge family relationships?

Enhances because:

Focus on Success

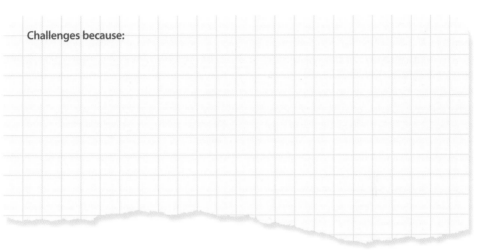

Challenges because:

3. To what extent does our family already focus on success?
   (What is my evidence, and where can we go from here?)

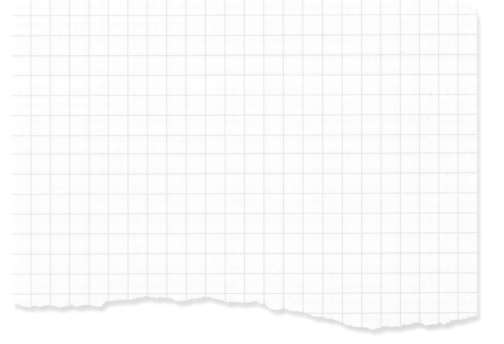

4. Do we currently hold family meetings? If so, how can we improve them? If not, how can we get started?

☐ Yes, we hold meetings   ☐ No, we do not currently hold meetings

Purpose

Parameters/Norms

Principles
(How will we address the following)

Reflective action

Authentic engagement

Appreciative inquiry

Focus on Success

Grounded vision

Adaptive confidence

Detached interdependence

Responsible freedom

Tough love

Priorities
(Where will we start, and what will be our timeline?)

Focus on Success

Other notes:

Focus on Success

DIFFERENTIATING BETWEEN ART AND ARCHITECTURE

Differentiating Between Art and Architecture

Are you traditional or visionary? Do you believe that children inherit who they are or learn behaviors and attitudes from the people around them? Or do you find these questions to be unfair, too black and white? Human architecture is not about creating your child masterpiece. That is art. Architecture is about helping would-be homeowners design the Color home that suits them. It requires parent architects to listen, to guide, and to support what they believe their children can become when they build on the strengths of their Color rainbow. Parent architects model adaptive confidence. They apply their skills and experience to help their children grow, but they are willing to adapt what they know about life to suit their children's unique temperament.

In this chapter we consider how parents can apply human architectural skills to guide and support children rather than trying to be artists focused on creating their own masterpiece – the perfect child. Architects can get more from prospective clients when they focus on the clients' beliefs and values rather than trying to shape them. At the same time, they must bring their specialized skills to the table. Skilled architects know how to balance their skills with their clients' needs. The same is true for parent architects. Figure 5.1 illustrates how you can bring your knowledge of Colors to the table to help your children balance their desire for comfort with their need to meet local building codes.

Differentiating Between Art and Architecture

Balancing Personal Comfort With Building Codes
Figure 5.1

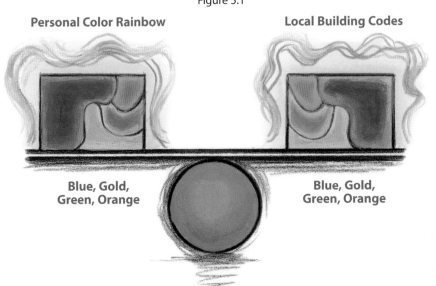

Personal Color Rainbow

Local Building Codes

Blue, Gold,
Green, Orange

Blue, Gold,
Green, Orange

As children try to design their Color home, they confront various building codes: family codes, friends' codes, school codes, community codes, etc. As a parent architect you can help your children learn to balance their desire for personal comfort (being their Color) with their need to follow local building codes (doing all the Colors).

Designing a Color home is similar to designing any other home. Your children need to develop a sense of control over the design process. You can help your children learn to balance personal comforts with local building codes by openly discussing how you and other family members filter your decisions through your Color rainbow. Hartzler and Henry's four steps described in the last chapter (1994) can provide a useful guide to this modeling process:

- *Identify & prioritize family needs*
- *Clarify expectations for a family win-win*
- *Understand individual and family strengths and liabilities*
- *Take responsibility for established family values, beliefs, and priorities*

This kind of balance does not occur naturally in any family. It must be consciously designed and consistently supported. This requires parent architects to make connections within the family that celebrate differences by asking the Four-P questions described earlier:

- *Why is this important?*
- *What are the rules of the game?*
- *How will I make this work?*
- *Will it make a difference?*

Where are you and your children relative to this balancing act? Your children can develop a more balanced approach to designing their own Color home by learning to ask the Four-P questions within your family. Most people are more comfortable doing the things they enjoy rather than doing the things that other people expect of them. How can you manage the architectural design tasks in ways that allow your children to be who they are without ignoring other people's needs as well as various local building codes?

Differentiating Between Art and Architecture

Your children will learn to trust you and to overlook minor indiscretions when they believe that you value and respect their Color rainbow. They will follow your advice when you help them realize their expectations. Build on their strengths. Let's reflect a moment on the five architectural guidelines that form the foundation for this book.

1. *Know what quality architecture looks like.*

2. *Ask the homeowner questions and listen to the answers.*

3. *Know the building codes in your community.*

4. *Focus on the homeowner's strengths and apply your skills to enhance them.*

5. *Manipulate your drawings rather than manipulating the homeowner.*

We have already discussed the first four steps in this human architectural process. Let's shift our focus to the fifth and final step: manipulating your drawings rather than manipulating the homeowner.

Creating Architectural Drafts

If you want your children to develop the balance described in Figure 5.1, you need to help them understand the roles and responsibilities within your family structure. These roles and responsibilities should evolve from their strengths and be developed toward a balance among all four Colors – be your Color, but do all the Colors. As the architect, you need to help your children learn to see how their Color strengths can help them solve a particular task and how they can sharpen their skills in those areas that are not as strong. An architectural contract outlined in Figure 5.2 may help you plan specific tasks so that they become learning experiences for your children.

Developing Architectural Guidelines
Figure 5.2

Reflective Action	What is the Color rainbow that describes your child's temperament, and how might the strengths and liabilities of your child's rainbow help or hinder achievement of this task?
Authentic Engagement	How much experience and what level of maturity does your child bring to this task, and where can you provide assistance?
Appreciative Inquiry	What are the critical questions that need to be answered in this situation?
Grounded Vision	What are realistic goals given your child's experience and maturity relative to the task at hand?
Adaptive Confidence	What are the results you and your child prefer and what could you both live with?
Detached Interdependence	How will you and your child divide responsibilities so that you are assisting with the task but not completing it for your child?
Responsible Freedom	What are the expectations you and your child have for one another during this task?
Tough Love	How will you and your child assess the value of this experience both in short-term results and long-term learning?

Differentiating Between Art and Architecture

You and your children can use these guidelines to plan growth experiences. But be careful not to turn this positive, practical tool into a boring drudgery. Remember, your children will learn more from your actions than from your words. The purpose of architectural guidelines is to provide a common vocabulary through which you and your children can communicate.

As you prepare to implement the guidelines, think about the Workable Space diagram presented in Figure 5.3. This diagram can be particularly helpful in dealing with disagreements with your children. But it can be used more proactively as a planning and discussion tool.

Workable Space Diagram
Figure 5.3

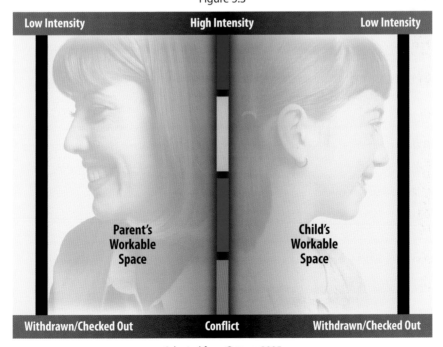

Adapted from Ortega, 2005

Differentiating Between Art and Architecture

The black line on the left side of the diagram represents the parent's line of low intensity, the point at which the parent in any situation is withdrawn or checked out. The black line on the right side represents the child's line of low intensity, the point at which the child is withdrawn or checked out. The multicolored dotted line in the center represents a line of high intensity that indicates conflict.

Think about the concept of being your Color but learning to do all of the Colors. If you are interacting with your child, you need to be aware of the potential for conflict. However, it is not always a good idea to avoid conflict. Instead you may want to manage the conflict to your mutual advantage. Conflict is often little more than a difference of perceptions.

Consider any interaction with your child. Prior to the initiation of the interaction neither of you is attentive to the other. You could be said to be withdrawn or checked out. If you are comfortable in the given situation, you can each remain in your workable space. If you have differences, however, one or both of you may move toward the high intensity line where there will be conflict. If either you or your child pushes toward the high intensity line, the other can choose to engage in conflict or withdraw. The trick to dealing with most conflicts is to remain in your workable space, neither pushing too close to the high intensity line nor withdrawing toward the low intensity line. Knowing the Color from which your child approaches a problem with you and the Color through which you might tend to respond can help you diffuse a conflict.

Differentiating Between Art and Architecture

For example, if your child's primary Color is blue, you might remain calm within your workable space, responding to your child through his or her Color rather than reacting through your Color. A Gold response to a Blue initiative may seem judgmental rather than helpful. "I don't think it is your responsibility (Gold) to take care of your friend's problem (Blue)." Look for the Color through which the exchange has been initiated and respond to that initiative – do the Color even if it is not your preferred Color.

Fourteen-year-old Felicia wanted to go to a party that would include seventeen and eighteen-year-olds, but she knew her mother would not approve. She approached the situation as a conflict through her natural preference for Blue. *"Mom, you say you trust me, and I want to believe you. But you never let me go to parties with older kids, kids like Jamie and Connor who go to our church. Since you seem to be more comfortable when I hang with kids from church, don't you think you need to trust me and trust them more?"*

At this point Miranda has several options. She can withdraw and capitulate to Felicia's manipulation, or she can reprimand her for having "brought up a closed subject." Or Miranda could stay in her workable space by doing Blue. *"You are so correct, Felicia, that I trust both you and your friends from church. In fact, I trust most of the kids that are going to be at this party. But this is not an issue of trust. It is a matter of age and experience. Given the relatively short lifespan of everyone involved here, three or four years makes a great deal of difference. I'd be more than happy to have you interact with these kids at a party at church where there would be several adults to monitor and guide everyone. I just care too much about all of you to place you in a situation where a silly, unintended mistake could place you in a compromising situation that could have long-term consequences."*

Miranda's response to Felicia's manipulative challenge allowed her to stay in her workable space. Because it was not challenging or combative, it also allowed Felicia to decide whether or not to return to her workable space. Felicia could leave her mother's space without losing face.

Keirsey's research (1998) indicates that less than 10% of the overall population turn automatically to rational thinking as a way to solve problems. Forty to forty-five per cent of the population (Golds) approach problem solving from a perspective of "doing what they do better." Another 35-40% experiment until something works.

The overall process of problem solving is rational or Green. But it emerges through all of the Colors. The real question here is one of purpose, "Why is attending this party important to Felicia?" The next question is a parameters question, "What rules do we have and why do they exist?" Then Felicia and Miranda can consider the principles question, "Is there any middle ground that can allow Felicia to achieve her purpose without jeopardizing her safety and well-being?" Finally, the priorities question emerges, "Is there or is there not a workable solution?"

Differentiating Between Art and Architecture

Sometimes your children's lack of experience or maturity may not allow them to see the logic behind your decision. However, it is not usually productive to "shut them down." Instead of saying, "We've discussed this before, and we are not going to discuss it again," you might say, "Explain to me what has changed since the last time we discussed this issue."

Influencing Learning Rather Than Dictating A Solution

Your effectiveness as a parent-architect depends more on influence than on authority. You can require your children's temporary compliance, and often time and circumstances leave you no other choice. But to gain their respect and to encourage them to adopt the Four-P habits, you should try to walk them through the process – model behaviors that you want them to learn.

You cannot wait until a moment of conflicting purposes, however, to begin your modeling process. As a parent-architect, you can work out local building codes as your children progress from one situation to another. What might have been different in Felicia and Miranda's discussion if they had constructed a set of parameters and guiding principles before Felicia left middle school and entered the high school?

As your children mature, they can take on more responsibility for decisions regarding their Color home design. You need to build your children's decision making capacity over time. They may not be able to master every skill they need to complete a task to your satisfaction, but you can communicate

Differentiating Between Art and Architecture

clear guidelines for your needs and expectations. And the more mature your children become, the more you can communicate the logic behind those decisions.

A good way to develop a balance in your relationship with your children is to discuss your Color characteristics – how they match up or compliment one another. Can your children recognize and appreciate their own Four-P tendencies? Do they recognize the strengths and liabilities their Color rainbow presents in various situations? Even when their Color preferences don't match the task at hand, have they learned to do all of the Colors?

Let's take a look at Shane who is Green-Gold. Shane does quite well academically in school, but he is a hard person to like. From kindergarten through fourth grade, teachers have reprimanded Shane for being rude and condescending to classmates and adults. Few children like to play with Shane at recess, and no one wants to work in a study group or team with him. Each year his teachers have met with Shane's parents to correct his behavior. From kindergarten through second grade, Mr. and Mrs. Breszinski tried to work with Shane's teachers, but for the past couple of years they have taken a more resistive attitude toward the school. Lately Mrs. Breszinski has become almost hostile. She seems to resent the fact that the school cannot accept her son as different. *"He is a bright young man much like his father,"* she insists. *"I'm tired of the other children bullying him and angry that school officials seem to blame Shane for all the problems. Perhaps I need to hire a lawyer,"* she says in an exasperated tone.

Then enters Mrs. Browne, Shane's fifth grade teacher. Prior to the first day of school, she had called Mrs. Breszenski to ask for a meeting with Shane, Mr. Breszenski, and herself. Her purpose was to get to know Shane so that she could help him have a better school year. *"I want to help Shane make friends and get on the right foot before his class moves to the middle school,"* she had told Mrs. Breszenski. *"If I can talk with the three of you, I think we can make this a better year for Shane. And I think Shane might feel better talking about this at home since school has not always been a pleasant place for him."*

Differentiating Between Art and Architecture

A twenty-year teaching veteran, Mrs. Browne has a reputation for high academic and behavior expectations. She is also recognized as a person who can get the best from her students. After exchanging pleasantries with Shane and his parents, Mrs. Browne thanks them for allowing her to meet with them and very directly states her purpose.

"I've come here tonight to get to know Shane and you and to decide how we can make this a great year for you at school, Shane. I'd like to begin by asking you what your goal is for this year, Shane."

"Well, my goal is to not have the other kids pick on me," Shane offers somewhat defiantly.

"I can assure you that no one will pick on you, Shane. But that is not really a goal. A goal is something that you want for yourself. It is about you as a person. What do you like and what do you want to learn?"

"Shane likes science and math like his father, but he can't enjoy those subjects when the other children make fun of him for being intelligent," Mrs. Breszenski adds.

"Do you like science and math, Shane?" Mrs. Browne inquires.

"I like them at home, but I hate them at school. I get bored with how childish they are and I get frustrated with the other kids who don't even try to figure out math and science problems. In groups I do all the work while the other kids visit with their friends. Then they take credit for my work and don't even understand how to present it without making stupid mistakes."

"That must be frustrating to do all the thinking and then be taken advantage of. But let's get back to setting goals. Goals are about personal growth. How do you want to grow as a learner and as a person? What kind of a person do you think you are now and what kind of person do you want to become?"

Differentiating Between Art and Architecture

Mrs. Browne pulls a diagram of Covey's *Circle of Influence and Circle of Concern* (1989) from her papers. She explains that the only control we have is control of our thoughts and actions. Then she explains that we can exercise influence over other people in some ways but that it is counterproductive to think that we can change them.

"You can waste a great deal of time worrying about the way other people act, or you can try to influence their behavior when it affects you. You probably can't change them, but you might influence the way they act with you," Mrs. Browne suggests. "You are a very bright young man with a great deal to share with your classmates. I'd like to help you understand yourself and your classmates better so that you can continue to do well academically and perhaps make some friends at the same time."

Mrs. Browne explains that she is not as scientific as the Breszenskis but that classrooms are not exactly laboratories. "These **Real Colors**® cards help me understand people and help me work from their strengths. Human beings are complicated."

Recognizing that Mr. Breszenski is a somewhat skeptical scientist, Mrs. Browne shares several pages of research studies about temperament. After about a half-hour of discussions around the cards, Mrs. Browne learns that Mr. Breszenski is a Green-Gold like Shane, and Mrs. Breszenski is a Gold-Green. She shares her own Color rainbow and describes how other people process and act on information. Then she explains how she uses her knowledge of **Real Colors**® to build positive relationships and a positive learning environment within her classroom. She uses the chart in Figure 5.4 to make her point.

Real Colors® in the Classroom
Figure 5.4

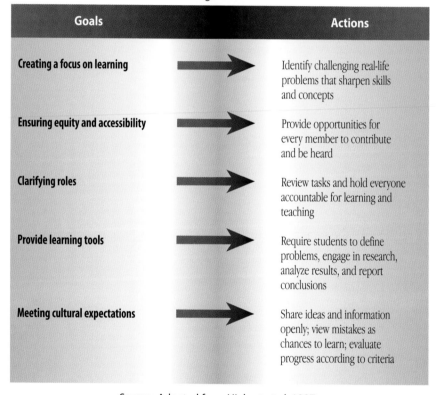

Goals	Actions
Creating a focus on learning	Identify challenging real-life problems that sharpen skills and concepts
Ensuring equity and accessibility	Provide opportunities for every member to contribute and be heard
Clarifying roles	Review tasks and hold everyone accountable for learning and teaching
Provide learning tools	Require students to define problems, engage in research, analyze results, and report conclusions
Meeting cultural expectations	Share ideas and information openly; view mistakes as chances to learn; evaluate progress according to criteria

Source: Adapted from Hiebert et al, 1997.

"In your father's work, he not only has to solve problems. He has to communicate and work with other people. There are probably times when he gets frustrated with his colleagues or his supervisors, but he needs to work with them in order to create new products. He cannot be required to like all his colleagues, but he is required to work effectively with them. That is how your father's company gets the most from him and how he gets to pursue the work that he loves. If he didn't love his work, these frustrations might not be worth it. The same is true in our classroom, Shane. And together we are going to work on how you can get the most out of your experience at school. If we work together on this, by the end of September I guarantee that you will be enjoying school and will have made at least two new friends. Are you willing to do your part?"

We won't take the time to run through Quinn's eight "take charge of your life" characteristics as they relate to this situation with Mrs. Browne and Shane. But can you identify examples of each: *reflective action, authentic engagement, appreciative inquiry, grounded vision, adaptive confidence, detached interdependence, responsible freedom, and tough love?*

Mrs. Browne concludes her visit to Shane's home by asking Shane once again to state a goal for the fifth grade year. She then shares Miller's *Question Behind the Question* (2004) concept of personal responsibility.

Differentiating Between Art and Architecture

"Shane, I can only control myself. Everything else is about influence. You can take charge of your life by taking personal responsibility for what happens in fifth grade. I'm ready to help you take charge, and I think your parents are willing to help too. Now what is your goal, that thing that you want most over the next year?"

"I want to have friends – real friends," Shane whispers.

"Now there is a goal," Mrs. Browne says as she picks up her papers.

Before leaving Mrs. Browne asks Shane and his parents to fill out the chart that appears in Figure 5.5. She has filled-in the first column based on their conversation. Mrs. Browne explains that working as a team requires all team members to contribute from their areas of strength. Since this is Shane's life, Mrs. Browne explains that he will take the lead in designing his Color home. She explains that she and Shane's parents will play supporting roles when they have Color strengths similar to Shane. Since Mrs. Browne is the only member of the team who has Blue as an area of strength, she will take a lead role in bringing Blue to their team effort. She asks the family to think of someone they respect who has Orange as a primary Color. Then she asks them to fill in the chart over the next week and to bring it to Shane's "Back to School Night." They will take a few minutes at the end of that event to set their first month's action plan.

Differentiating Between Art and Architecture

Take a look at Figure 5.5. Think about Shane's goal of having "real" friends. What commitments might each member of the team make to lead or support in each area. Notice the commitments that Shane and his parents have made. If their greatest strengths are also their greatest liabilities, what challenges does this team face?

A Rainbow Starting Place
Figure 5.5

| | Team Rainbow | | Commitments | |
	Strength	Liability	Leadership	Support
Blue	Mrs. Browne	Shane, Mom, Dad		
Gold	Shane, Mom, Dad, Mrs. Browne			
Green	Shane, Mom, Dad	Mrs. Browne		
Orange		Shane, Mom, Dad, Mrs. Browne		

Differentiating Between Art and Architecture

Shane's goal involves personal relationships, a Blue strength. This is an area of strength for Mrs. Browne. Since she, Shane, and both parents share a Gold strength, Mrs. Browne recognizes that she must make the classroom a safe, predictable environment. Mrs. Browne also recognizes that she must build on Shane's Green problem solving strengths. But since none of the team members has a strong Orange component, Mrs. Browne will need to rely on other people to supply the thrill and excitement in the classroom – not exactly a characteristic that is lacking among most ten-year-olds.

Shane's experience provides a good example of how parent-architects might need to seek help from other building experts such as teachers, coaches, scout leaders, etc. In talking with Shane's teachers from previous grades, Mrs. Browne learned that Shane never wanted to be a leader. While Shane never was at a loss to provide advice to leaders and always frustrated with what he saw as their inability to think logically, he preferred to avoid the spotlight. How might Mrs. Browne encourage growth in this area?

Obviously she needs to get Shane into a leadership role. But she cannot make him a leader, and none of her class is going to choose Shane to lead their group. Mrs. Browne must first create a safe environment in the classroom for Shane to practice his leadership skills. For Shane this is an Orange task. It is a challenge. He has the Green problem solving skills necessary to lead a meaningful task analysis. He has the Gold organizational skills to carry out the investigation. But he lacks both the relationship skills and the risk

Differentiating Between Art and Architecture

taking skills required in this situation. Let's see how Mrs. Browne and Shane's parents can support Shane in his leadership debut.

To build the relationships, Mrs. Browne leads a class discussion about group expectations. She explains that they are going to be a community of learners whom she cannot force to be good friends but whom she will expect to be respectful and inclusive of everyone.

When parents and other significant adults react favorably to different "personalities" over time, they model appropriate learning for children. Children can learn to appreciate an Orange's sense of risk-taking, a Blue's sensitivity in a social setting, a Green's ability to be objective, and a Gold's ability to organize and complete a task. But they also need to understand that each Color has its liabilities.

By visiting the Breszenski home, Mrs. Browne has made it safe for Shane and his parents to take a risk. Their history with school has been a series of primarily negative experiences. Therefore, Mrs. Browne recognizes that she must take the first step. She uses her Blue strength to build a relationship with the entire Breszenski family. By appreciating their needs, she has modeled relationship building and risk taking for Shane and his parents. But she has also set expectations for their future participation in this process. They have established a shared purpose, agreed on a common focus for Shane's yearly goal, and begun to reflect on their team strengths. Mrs. Browne has also established a framework from which each team member can take personal responsibility for leading or supporting Shane toward achieving his goal.

A shared commitment can fade quickly when the team experiences stress. It can fade even more quickly if you fail to define tasks clearly or to clarify roles and responsibilities. Growth requires patience and perseverance. It requires an understanding of building a set of plans (a commitment to a common purpose), a need to understand the local building codes (in this case classroom culture), designing a method to monitor progress and provide feedback, and a willingness to take a risk even when past experiences have not been positive or successful.

It takes time to shift our focus from what Peale (1974) calls the 3-L's – lack, loss, and limitation – to an assets model of learning and development where we can appreciate our own as well as other people's strengths. This shift will never be easy and will usually require parent-architects to rely on other people for advice and support. You will have neither the time nor the energy to analyze your children's lives on a daily basis. But when you encourage your children to take part in the process and you take the time to give them meaningful feedback on their progress, you will be modeling the kinds of attitudes and behaviors you want them to demonstrate.

Let's return a moment to the *Real Relationships Table*. The menu that appears on page 156 is as applicable to parent-child relationships as it is to adult-adult relationships. Figure 5.6 repeats the concepts from the

Real Relationships Menu. As parents we can become so involved with our parental responsibilities that we lose sight of the common courtesies that are so normal among adults. Notice that the menu has been adapted for use by parents to build a working relationship with their children.

The Parent's Real Relationships Menu
Figure 5.6

Appetizer
Making your children feel comfortable
in their own Color home
Complimenting what to you seems small
but to them may be significant
Asking follow-up questions to
show that you truly care

Soup or Salad
Finding out your children's preferences
Offering your children choices
Connecting what you like to what they like

Entrees
Giving them chances to focus the conversation
Providing your own examples of
similar challenges and successes
Your choice of serious or funny, or a bit of each.

Dessert
I've had a wonderful time talking with you
You have so many interesting experiences
Let's do this again

Making Connections

You can help your children create a strong, balanced Color home by helping them see the connections from one experience to another. Figure 5.7 provides a rubric or method for evaluating how your children's actions compare to their personal goals and expectations. It helps them develop their ability to reflect on their daily experiences in relationship to their long-term goals.

To use the chart, you should first ask your children what kind of person they want to be. Remember, don't focus on a goal of improving a liability. Focus first on what they do well. Then ask them how they know they can do that well. You might then ask them what they hope to be able to do in the future. For younger children this may be a matter of weeks or months. For older children and adolescents, you may need to expand their thinking to a longer period of time. Nevertheless, it is important to remember that even a fourteen-year-old has a difficult time thinking clearly about adult goals. To younger adolescents it seems like an eternity until they can drive. How can they think realistically beyond high school graduation?

As you look at this *Human Architectural Rubric*, can you anticipate how your children might answer your questions differently according to their age and level of maturity? Ask yourself what a mature (fill-in the year)-year-old might look like. Then ask yourself what a mature (fill-in the Color) (fill-in the year)-year-old might look like.

Differentiating Between Art and Architecture

Human Architectural Rubric
Figure 5.7

	Exemplary	Satisfactory	Needs Improvement	Unacceptable Must be Revised
Personal goals or expectations				
Recently demonstrated behaviors or attitudes				
Alignment with personal goals or expectations	Behaviors are consistently aligned with personal goals and expectations.	Behaviors are sometimes aligned with personal goals and expectations.	Behaviors are frequently not aligned with personal goals and expectations.	Behaviors are seldom aligned with personal goals and expectations.
Plans for future				
Support you want from others				

Differentiating Between Art and Architecture

If you want your children to find this rubric useful, don't use it as a hammer. Make it a positive tool. Laugh with them. Share your mistakes with them. Seek their help in assessing your growth. Show them how to self-evaluate and model how to provide positive feedback and suggestions rather than criticisms. Model how to accept and apply constructive criticism.

As your children get into the habit of developing personal goals and expectations and receiving feedback on their progress, they will begin to elevate their reflection from pleasing you to satisfying their own expectations for growth. Managing day-to-day attitudes and behaviors toward personal growth is a life-long undertaking. Effective parent-architects model effective management. They teach their children more than appropriate behaviors. They teach them the underlying principles that connect their daily actions with their personal goals. They teach them to set priorities and to recognize that good habits are every bit as easy to develop as bad habits. And in so doing, they encourage their children to become personally accountable for their own lives.

Success breeds success, but it also elevates expectations. When your children realize that they can have a positive impact on their world, they will no longer be satisfied with the status quo. Don't build your children's Color home. Help them design it. Be a parent-architect rather than a parent-artist. You have, to some degree or another, designed your Color home. Help your children design a home that is right for them, one that can grow with them.

Intimacy is not always found in someone who thinks and acts as we do. More often it is found in someone who completes us, who brings balance

Differentiating Between Art and Architecture

into our lives, and who finds balance in knowing and interacting with us. Lasting intimacy comes with honesty and self-disclosure. It comes from taking shared responsibility for successes and setbacks rather than ascribing blame. It comes from sensitivity to one another's needs. It comes from caring enough to plan for the future together, to struggle together in the face of impossible odds, and to stay focused on a common purpose that is greater than either person.

Intimacy is not found. It grows. As a parent-architect you need to become intimately familiar with your children's needs and interests. Guide and support them, but give them room to become all that they can be. Learn to call on engineers and contractors, like Mrs. Browne, who can help you turn your child's plans into reality. Teach them how to evaluate effective contributors to their dreams and to recognize the reality of local building codes. Listen to them and value what they say, and they will learn to listen to you and value what you say.

Growth is not about a single action or event. The magic lies in the connections that you and your children build between and among your goals and expectations for yourselves and each other. The more consistently your children meet their own expectations over time and across situations, the closer they will come to owning the Color home that is right for them. The more intimately involved they are in designing that home, the more willing they will be to assume accountability for their actions.

Differentiating Between Art and Architecture

In the final chapter we will examine the demands that architectural expectations place on parents and how you can apply the five steps described in this book within various situations. But first, take a moment to reflect on the items on the next couple of pages. Ask yourself how closely your words and actions match your personal values and commitments.

Artist or Architect?

1. Would you describe yourself as a parent-architect or a parent-artist? What evidence do you have to make this judgment?

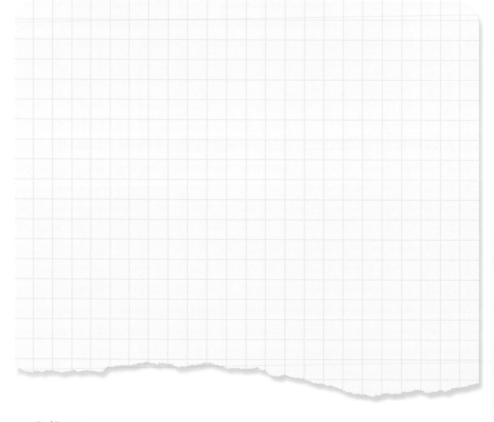

Differentiating Between Art and Architecture

2. How do you balance your personal comfort with local building codes? Is this an effective model for your children?

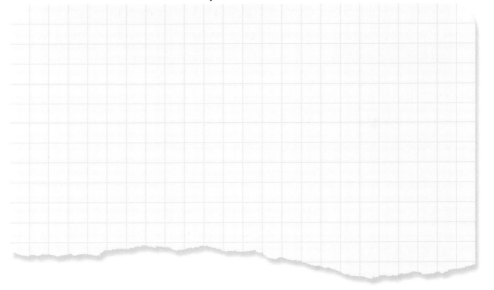

3. How have you developed architectural guidelines with your children?

Differentiating Between Art and Architecture

A Plan for Architectural Guidelines	
Reflective Action	How might the strengths and liabilities of your child's rainbow help or hinder Color home design?
Authentic Engagement	How do you provide assistance to your child's home design?
Appreciative Inquiry	What critical questions do you routinely ask your children?
Grounded Vision	What are your child's goals and how realistic are they?
Adaptive Confidence	How do you model adaptive confidence for your children?
Detached Interdependence	Who leads and who supports in what situations?
Responsible Freedom	How do you make it safe for your children to fail?
Tough Love	How do you model tough love?

Differentiating Between Art and Architecture

4. How do you and your children communicate about your workable spaces?

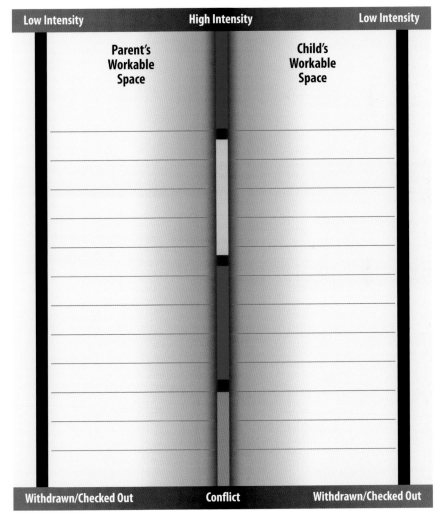

Workable Space Diagram

Low Intensity	High Intensity	Low Intensity
Parent's Workable Space		Child's Workable Space

| Withdrawn/Checked Out | Conflict | Withdrawn/Checked Out |

5. How might you adapt Mrs. Browne's *Real Colors Classroom* for use at home?

Real Colors® in the Classroom

Goals		Actions
Creating a focus on learning	→	Identify challenging real-life problems that sharpen skills and concepts
Ensuring equity and accessibility	→	Provide opportunities for every member to contribute and be heard
Clarifying roles	→	Review tasks and hold everyone accountable for learning and teaching
Provide learning tools	→	Require students to define problems, engage in research, analyze results, and report conclusions
Meeting cultural expectations	→	Share ideas and information openly; view mistakes as chances to learn; evaluate progress according to criteria

6. What might your rainbow starting place with your child, your spouse, and another significant adult look like?

A Rainbow Starting Place

	Team Rainbow		Commitments	
	Strength	Liability	Leadership	Support
Blue				
Gold				
Green				
Orange				

Differentiating Between Art and Architecture

7. Use a specific set of behaviors or attitudes to complete the architectural rubric with one of your children.

Human Architectural Rubric

Personal goals or expectations				
Recently demonstrated behaviors or attitudes				
Alignment with personal goals or expectations	**Exemplary**	**Satisfactory**	**Needs Improvement**	**Unacceptable Must be Revised**
	Behaviors are consistently aligned with personal goals and expectations.	Behaviors are sometimes aligned with personal goals and expectations.	Behaviors are frequently not aligned with personal goals and expectations.	Behaviors are seldom aligned with personal goals and expectations.
Plans for future				
Support you want from others				

Differentiating Between Art and Architecture

8. Can you complete the timeline below?

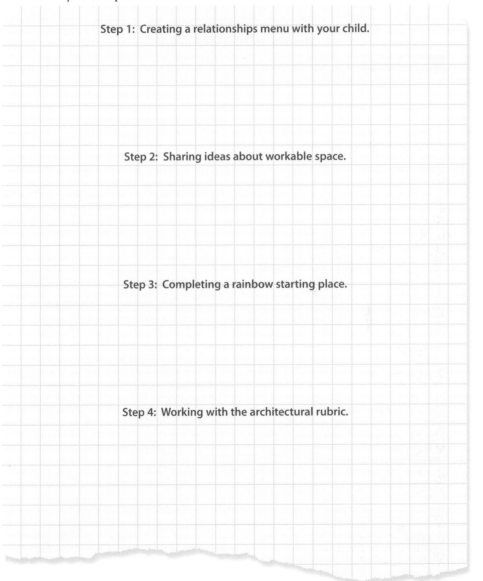

Step 1: Creating a relationships menu with your child.

Step 2: Sharing ideas about workable space.

Step 3: Completing a rainbow starting place.

Step 4: Working with the architectural rubric.

Differentiating Between Art and Architecture

Other notes:

Differentiating Between Art and Architecture

WORKING WITH COLOR CONTRACTORS

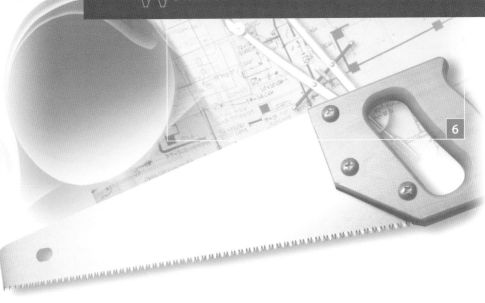

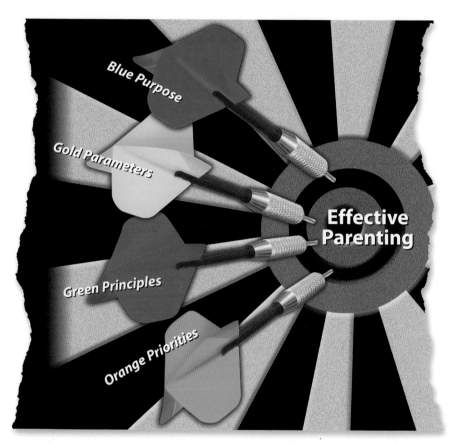

What does effective parenting look like, and how can you become a more effective parent-architect? Repeat after me, *"The most important thing to remember when it comes to parenting is that no one is perfect."* Now that wasn't hard to say. Was it? But as simple as this little mantra is to repeat, it is much more difficult to practice in our everyday lives as parent-architects.

Practicing effective parenting is a great deal like practicing darts. Your goal in darts is to come as close to the bull's eye as many times as you possibly can. You won't hit the bull's eye every time. It's your total score that counts in the end. The same is true for parenting. You will not be the perfect parent every day. And if you get caught-up in trying to play the perfect game, you will lose sight of your overall purpose – to establish a relationship with your children that brings joy and growth to both of you and to everyone around you as well.

Figure 6.1 lays out what I call "breaking ground for Color home construction." When an architect sits down with a client, both individuals understand that their ultimate goal is to build a home that meets the client's dreams and expectations within the scope of the architects skills and abilities. As you consider this chart, notice that the first two columns listed under the shaded area (Terms and Targets) show a comparison of Color and Four-P terms. The third column, architectural design, provides a means of applying the Colors and Four-P concepts to becoming an effective parent. These three shaded columns are connected. That is, Blue is the equivalent of Purpose. The terms Blue and Purpose deal with making personal connections. The Human Architectural Design column shows how you can apply your knowledge of personal relationships toward building a relationship with your children. Making personal connections with your clients (children) is the first step toward helping them build a home to suit their needs.

The column in the non-shaded area of the chart, on the other hand, is not presented in rows. Both sets of skills listed under Architectural Guidelines and Engineering Schematics are required to some extent in each aspect of Human Architectural Design. The Parent-Architectural Guidelines and the Engineering Schematics are strategies that run throughout the Colors and the Four-P's. These are skills and strategies that parent-architects use to work with their clients (their children) and to coordinate their work with other people who may eventually be employed to assist in the construction of the client's Color home based on the architectural plans.

Breaking Ground for Color Home Construction
Figure 6.1

Terms and Targets			Navigating Building Codes
Color	Four-P Equivalent	Human Architectural Design	Architectural Guidelines
Blue	Purpose	Making personal connections with your client	1) Know what quality architecture looks like 2) Ask the homeowner questions and listen to the answers 3) Know the building codes in your community 4) Focus on the homeowner's fundamental
Gold	Parameters	Enhancing the probability of working together to create a plan that works for your client	values and apply your skills to enhance them 5) Manipulate your drawings rather than the homeowner
Green	Principles	Exploring connections between the client's vision and the architect's skills	**Engineering Schematics** 1) Reflective action 2) Authentic engagement 3) Appreciative inquiry 4) Grounded vision
Orange	Priorities	Enhancing the possibilities of creating the client's dream home within existing codes and conditions	5) Adaptive confidence 6) Detached interdependence 7) Responsible freedom 8) Tough love

Working With Color Contractors

Let's use the concepts from Figure 6.1 to think about the many contractors and sub-contractors that you and your child might work with in developing a strong and effective Color home. You will interact with a number of these contractors for various purposes, but we will limit our considerations here to three major areas: family, school, and community.

Family as Contractors

One of the first major contractors that can help build an effective Color home for your children is your family. This includes your child's siblings as well as extended family members such as grandparents, uncles, aunts, and cousins. Generally, these family members are the first people outside you, the parents, who will play an important role in building your children's Color home.

Patrick is a Blue-Orange four-year-old who thinks his Pap-Pap Willis walks on water. Willis is a Green-Gold who was away at war until his own son, Bill (also a Green-Gold), was four-years-old. Perhaps this is why Willis, now a widower, has doted on Patrick for the past four years.

A few months ago Patrick's parents, Paul (Green-Orange) and Sarah (Blue-Orange) adopted Mike, a three-year-old Korean child who is Green-Gold. How might the parent-architects Paul and Sarah work with Pap-Pap Willis, and Uncle Bill to help construct Patrick and Michael's Color homes? And how might Patrick and Michael influence one another's thinking about what kind of Color home they want?

Let's start by looking at the two boys' primary Colors along side their parent-architects' Colors. Figure 6.2 lays out each Color rainbow from greatest strength at the top of the list to greatest liability at the bottom of the list. The dotted line in the middle of the chart represents that imaginary line separating strengths and liabilities. Although this is a bit of an over-simplification, it will allow us to manage our analysis of building possibilities.

Client-Architect Rainbows
Figure 6.2

Clients		Architects	
Patrick	Michael	Sarah	Paul
Blue	Green	Blue	Green
Orange	Gold	Orange	Orange
Green	Orange	Green	Blue
Gold	Blue	Gold	Gold

As you look at this chart, what are the opportunities presented by each person's strengths (preferred Color) on the first line? Remember, building an effective Color home depends on understanding the parent-architectural guideline.

1. *Know what quality architecture looks like.*

2. *Ask the homeowner questions and listen to the answers.*

3. *Know the building codes in your community.*

4. *Focus on the homeowner's fundamental values and apply your skills to enhance them.*

5. *Manipulate your drawings rather than the homeowner.*

Quality human architecture requires a balance. Build on your strengths, but learn to do all the Colors. Paul and Sarah might use the following questions to design an architectural plan with Patrick and Michael.

- *How might Sarah's Blue present a problem for fully developing Patrick's Color rainbow?*

- *How might Paul's Green present a problem for fully developing Michael's Color rainbow?*

- *How might Sarah's Blue present a communications challenge for Michael?*

- *How might Paul's Green present a communications challenge for fully developing Patrick's rainbow?*

- *As you look at all four individuals' greatest liabilities (bottom line), what potential challenges can you see emerging?*

What other questions or challenges come to your mind as you look at this chart? Consider the following:

Working With Color Contractors

- *Which child's Color rainbow points naturally toward an interest in science and mathematics?*

- *Which child's rainbow points more naturally toward an interest in literature and writing?*

- *What special obstacle does Michael face regarding his Color home design needs?*

- *What special obstacle does Patrick face regarding his Color home design needs?*

- *Which parent-architect is likely to be the most empathetic with which child?*

- *Where will the parent-architects be most likely to need help from family engineers and contractors?*

- *Which child might feel "out-of-sync" in this nuclear family? Why?*

- *What construction expertise might Pap-Pap Willis and Uncle Bill bring to these home building projects?*

(For possible answers see pages 201-202 at the end of this chapter.)

Understanding the community building codes within this family circle is actually not complicated either. The trick is for Paul and Sarah to help Pap-Pap Willis and Uncle Bill apply their strengths to supporting Patrick and Michael's Color balance. That is, Willis and Bill need to know that as human contractors they are building parts of Patrick and Michael's

Working With Color Contractors

Color houses, not trying to make up for missing pieces from their own Color homes. Pap-Pap Willis and Uncle Bill could offer their expertise in terms of supporting Michael's use of his Gold room and in helping Patrick find his way to his Gold room occasionally. Since Paul and Sarah do not have a great deal of Gold to share with their children, they may want to take advantage of these two contractors. Sarah has noticed that Pap-Pap Willis and Uncle Bill enjoy Patrick's sensitivity now, but she wonders how their skills will apply when Patrick and Michael reach school age.

Paul and Sarah could help Pap-Pap Willis and Uncle Bill to focus on the boys' fundamental values and apply their skills to enhance them. They could begin reflective conversations with Willis and Bill regarding the fact that they want Patrick and Michael to develop Color homes that are appropriate to their own needs and interests. For example, they might compliment Michael's Gold room and complement Patrick's rainbow where Gold is his least prominent Color. (To compliment is to recognize; to complement is to complete or balance.) They might ask Willis and Bill to engage authentically with Patrick, making certain that their Green-Gold comes across as complementary rather than as provocative or condescending. Perhaps they can remind Willis and Bill to ask appreciative questions to determine Patrick's goals and interests and to extend Michael's natural curiosity. Willis and Bill need to understand that Patrick sees the world from a global/people related perspective rather than a logical scientific perspective.

Working With Color Contractors

Together these parents and their extended family can demonstrate acceptance of all Colors by manipulating their architectural plans rather than manipulating Patrick and Michael's values. They can encourage and support Patrick and Michael so that they develop their own sense of adaptive confidence, detached interdependence, and responsible freedom. Sarah needs to avoid a tendency to fill Patrick's Blue room with all her Blue stuff. She and Paul both need to avoid overcrowding Patrick's Orange room. Likewise, Willis and Bill need to avoid crowding Michael's Green and Gold rooms with their Green and Gold stuff. Tough love insists on a Color balance. Having grown up with a Green-Gold father, Sarah might have a tendency to over-indulge Patrick's Blue or over-react to Michael's Green. Having also grown up with a Green-Gold father, Paul might underestimate the need for Gold in Patrick's life or overreact to Michael's need for structure.

Planning a Color home is more about evolution than revolution. Children learn more from modeling than from anything parents and relatives tell them. Parents and family members have learned to think about and interact with the world in ways that feel comfortable to them. Often they lose sight of or even resist other ways of thinking. Parents cannot ignore their own Color preferences, but they can be aware of their strengths and liabilities so that they avoid simply passing their preferences onto their children. Figure 6.3 provides some interesting reminders for parents and family members as they assist children in designing and constructing their Color homes.

Working With Color Contractors

Color Comparisons
Figure 6.3

*Golds know that, while Oranges wonder if. Golds need to find,
while Oranges hope to discover. Golds try to protect, while Oranges
try to win. Golds want to collect the best, while Oranges want to
collect the most. Golds seek the safest, while Oranges seek the fastest.*

*Blues need to feel, while Greens need to understand why.
Blues love to talk with friends, while Greens need time alone to think.
Blues enjoy a good friend, and a warm fire, while Greens
enjoy a good puzzle, and symphonic music.*

Adapted from: Johnson, 2005.

As a parent-architect you make a commitment to develop house plans
that suit your children's needs and interests. In so doing, you assume
responsibility for supervising family contractors who may participate in
your children's home construction. Contractors and sub-contractors can be
much more effective when they have an opportunity to discuss architectural
drawings with the architect. Parent-architects can translate the emotions,
beliefs, and values that their children may not be able to articulate to adult
family members.

Working With Color Contractors

Remember, chances are almost three to one that a family member's primary Color will be Gold or Orange. (Golds comprise 40-45% of the world; Oranges comprise 35-40%.) This can present numerous challenges for children who are either Blue or Green. Expecting a Gold or Orange grandparent to understand the needs of a Blue grandchild is like asking a carpenter to perform electrical contracting responsibilities. Appreciation of a Color is not synonymous with understanding.

But family members are not the only contractors involved in helping your children construct their Color homes. What other contractors or sub-contractors might you engage in this construction project? Let's consider a very influential and powerful human contractor – schools.

Schools As Contractors

Figure 6.4 illustrates the similarities and differences among Colors inside and outside the school walls.

A Comparison of Colors Inside and Outside the School Walls
Figure 6.4

	General Population	School Staff
Blue	8-18%	25-30%
Gold	45-50%	65-70%
Green	7%	<5%
Orange	35-40%	<5%

Working With Color Contractors

As you look at this chart, notice that Gold represents the greatest percentage of people either inside or outside the school walls. However, notice how disproportionate the percentage of Golds is inside our schools. Golds make up from 65-70% of the teachers and administrators in a school — almost a 15% greater proportion than occurs in the general population. Blues, who make up 8-18% of the general population, make up 25-30% of the school staff. Finally, among a typical school staff Greens and Oranges combined comprise 10% or less of the teachers and administrators in your child's school.

These percentages have serious implications for your children. Let's consider a few.

- *Gold children have a distinct advantage in most schools.*
- *Blue children may form relationships in early years, but they could fall behind if their Gold falls lower within their Color rainbow.*
- *Orange and Green children could be at risk in many school settings.*
- *Green children whose Gold is their secondary Color stand a better chance of success in schools than do their Green-Orange classmates.*

Let's consider how these conditions might affect Patrick and Michael. As a Blue-Orange Patrick is at risk in a school setting. While he has the ability to relate directly to 25-30% of his teachers, he does not display a Gold strength so important to survival in a school environment where listening to and following directions and rules is so important to success. Michael is a Green-Gold who will have a better chance than Patrick of navigating among the adults in his school. However, the more aloof nature of his Green may pose obstacles to his relationships with Blue teachers. So what are Paul and Sarah to do to enhance Patrick and Michael's success in school?

Remember, Paul and Sarah are human-architects. They are responsible for consulting with Patrick and Michael's teachers so that together they can help the boys construct a Color home that meets their needs and interests. Let's use our eight characteristics to establish a set of architectural drawings for Patrick and Michael's success in school.

1. Reflective Action

School personnel are caring people, but 65-70% of them have an established understanding of what a classroom should look like. This is a Gold class-room. In a Gold classroom children sit quietly, focus on what the teachers say or demonstrate, and work very hard to replicate what the teachers "teach" them. This is a process that works for Gold children and for many other children whose parents have taught them to be sensitive to Gold routines. But for a large percentage of children – Greens, Oranges, and to some extent Blues – this environment inside the school walls does not build confidence and often makes success allusive.

Your job as a parent-architect is to help your children navigate this Gold maze. And if you are a particularly dedicated parent-architect, your job is to convince the school-contractors that their job is to build a house that suits your children rather than forcing your children to live within a Color home that falls short of their needs and interests.

In terms of reflective action, Paul and Sarah need to prepare their children for the schools as they currently exist. They need to teach Patrick and Michael to adapt to the Gold environment within their school. Then they need to form a partnership with the boys' teachers. In forming this partnership Paul and Sarah need to make certain that the teachers see them as supportive. Golds are not mean or narrow-minded. They follow routines that work for them. Like all of us, they rely on what they know how to do.

2. Authentic Engagement

How can Paul and Sarah engage authentically with Patrick and Michael's teachers? First, they need to understand the teachers' Color rainbow. They might ask some of the following questions:

- *What are your expectations for learning and behavior in this classroom and how can I support this in school and at home?*

- *What do you want to know about my child's interests and what I know about his learning style?*

- *How can we as parents communicate our goals for our child as a learner and as a contributing member within this classroom and school?*

- *How can we communicate with one another to make my child's school experience positive?*

These questions form a commitment to a common purpose. They can help parents and teachers form an authentic relationship to promote a child's success as a learner and as a human being. Parents often assume that they should take a backseat in schooling. Don't forget, you are the architect who guides and promotes your child's growth from birth to maturity and beyond. Teachers and other school personnel provide an important professional service as contractors, but the most effective teacher can never know a child as well as an effective parent.

3. Appreciative Inquiry

The purpose of asking questions is not to trap a teacher. If you want to enlist a person's help, you need to be authentic. Ask questions that promote a partnership. Don't look for someone to blame. Ask what went right before asking what went wrong. Assume that mistakes are more likely a matter of miscommunications than a lack of commitment. Figure 6.5 illustrates how you can turn an inquiry into an appreciative inquiry.

From Inquiry to Appreciative Inquiry
Figure 6.5

Inquiry	Appreciative Inquiry
1. Patrick came home crying. What happened?	1a. Patrick seemed to have a problem today. Can you tell me what happened so I can support your expectations for him?
2. What's wrong with that Kelley kid? Is he a bully or something?	2a. Michael and the Kelley child seem to be having problems. Do you have any idea what the problem might be and how I can work with you and Michael to improve the situation?
3. Can you try to give clearer directions for homework? Patrick says he doesn't understand what he's to do.	3a. I'm working with Patrick on his attention skills. Do you have any suggestions about how we can help him focus to make certain he understands his homework assignments?

Notice that appreciative inquiry questions promote partnership and shared responsibility for solutions. They are not accusatory. Rather, they describe the situation as objectively as possible and ask the teacher for assistance. Parents do not need to be apologetic or to "take the teacher's side" in every situation. Partnerships don't have sides. In a partnership or authentic relationship, the child, the parent, and the teacher share responsibilities. Often children have difficulty articulating their needs and concerns and assume they need to form sides to protect their interests. But if you as a parent remember that you are the architect in this construction project, you need to serve as a guide and interpreter. You need to help your children solve their problems rather than relying on you to solve them. Before calling the teacher you may want to ask your children questions similar to those listed below.

- *What do you think the problem is?*
- *What do you think might be an acceptable solution in this situation?*
- *How did you try to achieve this solution?*
- *What were the results when you tried that?*
- *How would you like for me to help you?*
- *What will you be responsible for if I do that?*

As you ask appreciative questions, keep in mind that this is an opportunity for you to help your children develop problem solving skills. It is important that your inquiry leads toward realistic solutions in terms of your children's

Color strengths and maturity. Younger children may need more direction and support than older children, but all children can learn to express their needs and understand their limitations if their parent-architects keep the vision for success grounded.

4. Grounded Vision

A grounded vision takes its roots in the child. As the architect you may need to consider some factors beyond your child's Color strengths and maturity. Again, what are the building codes in this situation? Schools are relatively large organizations whose clients come from varying backgrounds. By their very nature schools promote Gold parameters. This is the way we do things around here so that we can manage our time to achieve the greatest good for the greatest number of children.

You need to ask yourself how much of a partner the teacher is willing to be. How much time should you realistically expect a teacher to take in this situation? How significant is this situation in the scheme of things – not to you, but to your child? The way you handle problem situations models problem solving for your children. Children need to understand time constraints, authority, and consequences. They need to develop a sense of priorities and an ability to see a situation in terms of the big picture. They need to learn that being right does not always mean winning the argument. They need to develop adaptive confidence beyond any one situation.

5. Adaptive Confidence

The first thing your children need to know about a school situation is that you plan to offer guidance and support as they work with teacher-contractors. They need to know that they can call on you for advice and that you will provide assistance when problems are too serious for them to handle alone. They need to learn that some teacher-contractors will be more or less flexible depending on their own Color rainbows, training, and experience. Children can learn to adapt to various situations, but consistency of purpose is non-negotiable. Success in school requires a common purpose – a purpose in which learning becomes a joy and a passion for everyone involved.

Figure 6.6 illustrates how you can use the Four-P questions to ensure that you, your child, and your child's teacher share a common purpose and that your daily actions are consistent with that purpose.

The Four-P's and Adaptive Confidence
Figure 6.6

1. Purpose	Why is this important for my child to know and be able to do?
2. Parameters	What will my child, the teacher, and I be doing if we accomplish this purpose, i.e., what will success look like?
3. Principles	How will we monitor, assess, and adjust our individual and group contributions toward this end?
4. Priorities	How will we make certain that we put our energy into strategies and plans that work?

The first question in Figure 6.6 implies the importance of having a common and significant purpose for learning. You need to understand not only what your children are responsible for learning but how that learning will transfer to other situations this year, next year, and in life outside the school walls. Once you have developed this commitment, you need to ask yourself what success might look like. What will my children be doing, what will I be doing, and what will the teacher be doing if this thing works? Having a common purpose is important, but having a common understanding of what success looks like is equally important. Partnerships work more effectively when everyone knows the target and understands how the score will be kept.

And when we pause to reflect on our progress, what will we do if we are not hitting the target? If your children aren't learning within the parameters you, the teacher, and your child agreed to, you can change one of two things – your purpose or your parameters. You can say, "This is too much for us to expect of this child at this time." Or you can say, " If we want this child to learn this, we need to change something that one or all of us are doing."

Finally, when you make the necessary adjustments in purpose or parameters, you need to think about what did and did not work. When we did X, we got the expected results. Let's figure out the implications of X so that we can apply our energies in effective and efficient directions in future situations.

6. Detached Interdependence

Working as partners can be very rewarding for children, parents, and teachers. However, it is important that all members of the partnership understand their responsibilities. As in a marriage, this is not a 50-50 (or 33-33-33) proposition. Each individual must be committed to doing whatever it takes to accomplish the goal. If one person lacks the ability or will in one situation, the other two must pick-up the slack. The child, the parent, and the teacher should ask themselves, "Who is responsible for learning?" And each person's answer should be, "I am."

When all parties take full responsibility for learning, there is no room for blame or faultfinding. "I am responsible for learning. If one or more members of the partnership cannot or will not fulfill their responsibilities, I will simply need to work harder. We can reflect on the strengths of the partnership later." This is the meaning of detached interdependence. It does not alleviate anyone of responsibility, but it does not allow time for excuses.

7. Responsible Freedom

If the partnership is effective, each member – child, parent, and teacher – will be meeting their responsibilities. Remember the parameters question from earlier. What will the child, the parent, and the teacher be doing if their plan is successful?

All members of the partnership are free to contribute to learning according to their own strengths. However, no member is free to shirk responsibilities. If what I contributed was not effective, I need to adjust my strategies so that I can contribute more effectively in the future. Responsible freedom means that I can be who I want to be, but I must do what I need to do to make the partnership successful.

Working With Color Contractors

Ultimately your children will be responsible for their own learning. But you cannot allow them to consider failure as an option. As Csikszentmihalyi's research suggests (1990), children will learn best when they know what is expected of them, when they believe that they have the ability to accomplish it, and when they receive regular feedback on their progress. Responsible freedom requires parents and teachers to take time to reflect with children, not only about their success but about how they accomplished it. Children cannot become responsibly free if they cannot think critically and creatively about learning and about themselves as learners.

As a parent you can do little things to reinforce this type of reflection. When your child brings home an assignment, you can ask some of the following questions:

- *What are you learning about?*
- *Why is this important for you to know?*
- *What do you already know about this?*
- *What resources do we have available for this task, and where can we find other resources?*
- *What will be your biggest challenge in completing this assignment?*
- *This looks interesting. How can I help?*

When your child completes an assignment, you might ask some of the following questions:

- *May I read your answers to this assignment?*
- *Was it as difficult/easy as you expected?*
- *Did you learn anything that surprised you?*
- *Where do you think the teacher will go with this from here?*

The questions you ask should be genuine and appreciative. They should result in more than a monitoring of your children's schoolwork. They should say, "I love to learn and to help other people learn, and I want you to share that enthusiasm for learning."

Before we move to a consideration of community members and groups as contractors, let's consider the eighth and final piece of our engineering schematics, tough love. This is an area that pulls the other seven areas together.

8. Tough Love

Tough love is not touchy-feely. That's what makes it so tough. As a parent-architect you have a tremendous responsibility to look beyond your own needs and interests in order to provide guidance and support for the building of your children's Color homes. Tough love requires you to ask tough questions of yourself, your children, and those contractors and sub-contractors who will assist you in the construction of these homes. Figure 6.7 illustrates some of the challenges of this task according to the four Colors.

Tough Love In Technicolor
Figure 6.7

Parent's Color	Potential Challenges
Blue	• Keeping peace at all costs (Don't push the child; don't question the teacher) • Seeing things through "rose-colored glasses" (my child can do no wrong) • A willingness to accept less than a child might achieve • A fear of or aversion to competition • Seeing the big picture at the expense of the details
Gold	• A desire to see things done my way • Relying on known strategies even when they don't fit circumstances • A focus on rules that may be inconsistent with purpose • A tendency to overlook what is in favor of what could have been • Seeing the details at the expense of the big picture
Green	• Analysis paralysis • A focus on logic at the expense of people and politics • A focus on process at the expense of results • Avoidance of conflict in favor of logic • Objectivity that may appear arrogant or aloof
Orange	• Needing to get things done at any cost • A drive for competition at the expense of people and politics • A tendency to take chances and to avoid people who won't • Seeing things in terms of winners and losers • Underestimating the cost of mistakes

If you think back to *The Homeowner's Guide*, you will remember that we tend to surround ourselves with people who have values and interests similar to our own. In the *Relationships Guide* we also considered how we sometimes choose friends or partners whose differences we admire. When it comes to parent-architecture, we need to practice the best aspects of both these approaches. After all, we don't choose nor can we change our children's Color rainbow.

As a parent-architect you must make a conscious effort to understand and appreciate your children's Color rainbow, use your strengths to enhance and deepen the quality of that rainbow, and bring your children into contact with people who can both compliment and complement their Color balance.

Tough love requires Blue parents to recognize their strengths relative to relationships without ignoring their liabilities relative to conflict. It requires Gold parents to recognize their strengths relative to organization and management without ignoring their liabilities relative to change or different paths to the same end. Green parents need to recognize their strengths relative to analysis and problem solving without ignoring their liabilities relative to analysis paralysis. And Orange parents need to recognize their strengths relative to adventure and risk taking without ignoring their liabilities relative to teamwork and competition.

It's okay to make inquiries at school if they are appreciative inquiries. It's okay to have high expectations for your children and their teachers if they evolve from a grounded vision. It's desirable for you to participate in your children's education when that participation is genuine, based on reflective action, and aimed at developing your children's adaptive confidence, detached interdependence, and responsible freedom. But none of these things is possible unless you are willing to approach your parent-architect responsibilities through tough love.

There are many contractors and subcontractors willing and able to help you apply your architectural drawings to construct an effective Color home to meet your child's needs. Let's take a look at a few more of these contractors as they may appear in your community.

Community Members and Groups As Contractors

To promote quality in any form, parent-architects must seek what Quinn (1996) calls "deep change." Rather than managing your children's lives, you need to manipulate your architectural skills in ways that promote opportunities for your children to develop a balanced Color rainbow. It is not enough to talk about living a balanced life. You must model this balance and reflect with your children about their own efforts to achieve such a balance in their lives.

Can you let go of enough of your past to help your children find success in their future? We live in a time of rapid change, a time that has led Thomas Friedman (2005) to suggest that the world is flat. That is, due to a meteoric surge in technology, our world and the beliefs and values that have guided our journey through it to date may no longer be adequate for our children in their future. Let's consider what this might mean to you as a parent-architect.

Technology now allows businesses to transfer work to workers. This means that your children will need to be much more adaptable than you had to be to be successful. As businesses offshore jobs, your children's jobs may not even have been invented yet. For example, when I was in high school, personal computers had not been invented. Therefore, there was no job called computer technician. There was no need for someone to service or create software for the Internet. What are the implications of these changes to your children's future? Where will the church, Boy Scouts, neighborhoods, and community centers fit into this future?

As the world becomes more and more accessible through technology, you may want to protect your children, to shield them from all the "bad" stuff out there. And of course, children do need our protection from the overabundance of violence and pornography in our world. But ask yourself, "Can I really shield my children from every potential threat, or would I be better advised to give them the guidance and support to protect themselves?"

With community contractors as with family and school contractors, you must remember that as the parent, you are the architect. Once again, the Four-P's provide a useful set of questions for screening community contractors to help construct your children's Color homes.

Working With Color Contractors

Purpose	*Why is this individual, group, or activity important to my children's development?*
Parameters	*What would my children, these individuals, groups, and activities, and I be doing if we accomplish this purpose?*
Principles	*How will I guide my children in monitoring and adjusting their participation with these individuals, groups, and activities?*
Priorities	*How will I guide my children's participation with community members, groups, and activities to help them gain the most effective Color balance possible?*

These are not esoteric questions. They are practical guides for parent-architects to use in evaluating community experiences with their children. Additional questions you might consider asking include the following:

- *How do my children's Color rainbow and experiences prepare them for this community contractor?*

- *Is this contract truly designed to meet my children's needs rather than my own needs?*

- *Is this contractor a compliment or a complement to my children's Color balance?*

- *Is this contractor likely to demand a stretch for my children? If so, how will I support them?*

- *Does the individual, group, or activity provide a growth opportunity for my children, or is it designed to be recreational?*

- *Does the individual, group, or activity share my purpose and values?*

- *How involved will I be with this contractor?*

- *How prepared are my children to assume contract responsibilities with this individual, group, or activity?*

Children can learn from any experience, but they can learn much more from experiences when they have a sense of purpose and control and are provided time to reflect openly and honestly about their experiences. How will you create this richness with your children?

It takes many people to build a Color home. Those people need to have a common purpose, an agreed upon set of decision making parameters, a process for monitoring their progress, and a plan for effectively allocating their energies. Parenting can be one of the most rewarding experiences of a person's life. To get the most from and to give the most to this experience, you should remember Kahil Gibran's admonition that children come through us, not from us. Whether you are about to embark on parenting for the first time or simply looking for ways to improve your parenting skills, think of yourself as an architect whose joy comes from helping a client (your child) build a Color home that will be unique, substantial, serviceable, and comfortable and will become an asset to the community.

Working With Color Contractors

Possible answers to questions on page 179.

- *Which child's Color rainbow points naturally toward an interest in science and mathematics?*

  Michael's rainbow. *Science and mathematics are more logically consistent disciplines that tend to attract Greens.*

- *Which child's rainbow points more naturally toward an interest in literature and writing?*

  Patrick's rainbow. *Literature and writing are more open, relational disciplines that tend to attract Blues.*

- *What special obstacle does Michael face regarding his Color home design needs?*

  Michael has a secondary Gold preference. *Gold is the last Color in his parents and Patrick's Color rainbow.*

- *What special obstacle does Patrick face regarding his Color home design needs?*

  Patrick's last Color is Gold, *like Paul and Sarah. Parents cannot pass on to their children something that they don't have.*

- *Which parent-architect is likely to be the most empathetic with which child?*

  Sarah and Patrick share a Blue preference *for seeing the world. Paul and Michael share Green.*

Working With Color Contractors

- *Where will the parent-architects be most likely to need help from family engineers and contractors?*
  In Gold areas, *the last Color in their rainbow.*
- *Which child might feel "out-of-sync" in this nuclear family? Why?*
  Michael. He has a secondary Gold *that no other nuclear family member shares.*
- *What construction expertise might Pap-Pap Willis and Uncle Bill bring to these home building projects?*
  They bring an adult concept of Gold.

Taking a Final Four-P Inventory

1. What is my vision of a quality school experience?

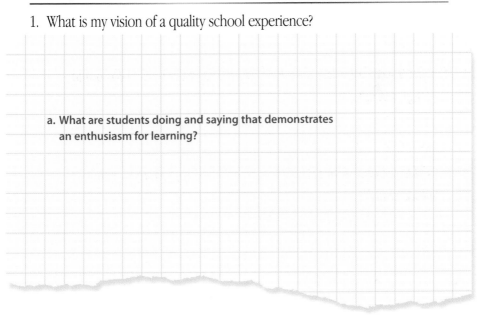

a. What are students doing and saying that demonstrates an enthusiasm for learning?

Working With Color Contractors

    b. How are parents and community members participating in our
       schools, and what are they saying about the quality of our schools?

    c. How are teachers talking about and planning for learning?
      Are they excited and enthusiastic or feeling overburdened?

    d. How are administrators encouraging inquiry and reflection
      through staff and community dialogues?

2. How have I used my vision of quality as a catalyst to encourage spirited discussions about the purpose of schooling?

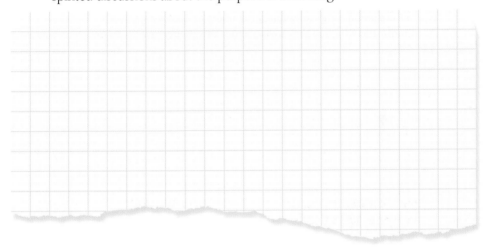

3. How do various stakeholders within my school community describe the atmosphere for change? Is it happening to them or with them?

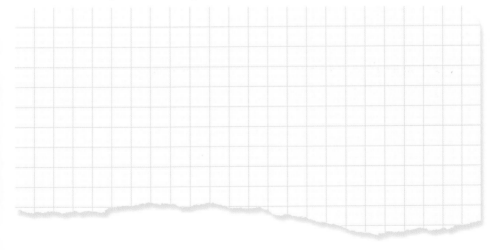

4. To what extent have we achieved the Four-P balance?

    a. Answering questions regarding programs and services in terms of what students need to know and be able to do.

    b. Listening to everyone, but listening more to those who have expertise or accountability in a particular area.

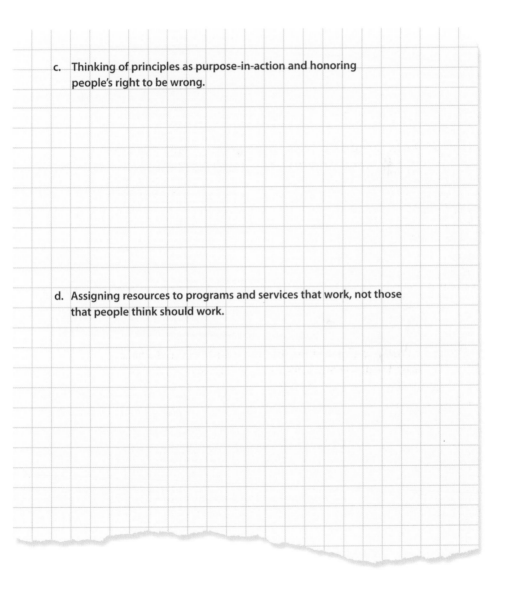

c. Thinking of principles as purpose-in-action and honoring people's right to be wrong.

d. Assigning resources to programs and services that work, not those that people think should work.

Working With Color Contractors

Other notes:

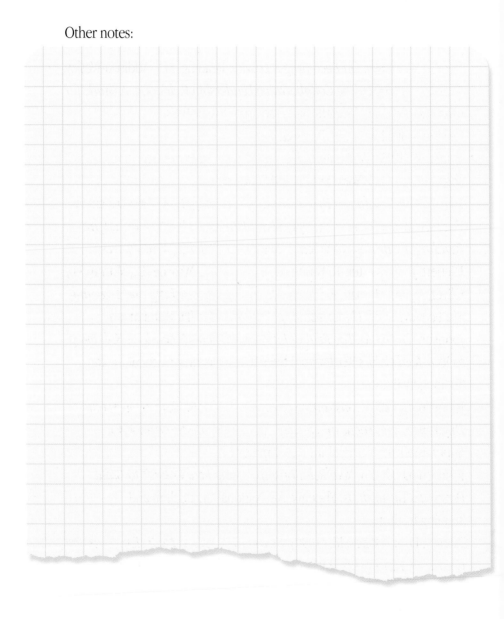

References

Bennis, W. (1989). *On Becoming A Leader.* Reading, MA: Addison-Wesley.

Chrislip, D. (2002). *The Collaborative Leadership Fieldbook: A Guide for Citizens and Civic Leaders.* San Francisco: Jossey-Bass.

Csikszentmihalyi, M. (1990). *Flow.* New York: Harper & Row.

Frankl, V. (1959). *Man's Search for Meaning: An Introduction to Logotherapy.* New York: Simon and Schuster.

Hart, L. (1983). *Human Brain, Human Learning.* New York: Longman.

Hartzler, M. and Henry, J. (1994). *Team Fitness: A How-to Manual for Building a Winning Work Team.* Milwaukee, WI: ASQ Quality Press.

Hiebert, J., Carpenter, T., Fennema, E., Fuson, K., Wearne, D., Murray, H., Oliver, A., and Human, P. (1997). *Making Sense: Teaching and Learning Mathematics with Understanding.* Portsmouth, NH: Heinemann.

Johnson, D. (2004). *The Real Colors® Homeowner's Guide: A Follow-up to Your Real Colors Workshop.* Phoenix, AZ: National Curriculum and Training Institute.

Johnson, D. (2005). *Sustaining Change in Schools: How to Overcome Differences and Focus on Quality.* Alexandria, VA: Association for Supervision and Curriculum Development.

Johnson, D. (2006). *Real Relationships: Using Real Colors® to Build Personal Connections.* Phoenix, AZ: National Curriculum and Training Institute

Keirsey, D. and Bates, M. (1998). *Please Understand Me II: Temperament, Character, Intelligence.* Del Mar, CA: Prometheus Nemesis Books.

References

Kroeze, D. and Johnson, D. (1997). *Achieving Excellence: A Report of Initial Findings from the Third International Mathematics and Science Study.* Northbrook, IL: First in the World Consortium.

Lieberman, A. and Grolnick, M. (1997). *"Networks, Reform, and the Professional Development of Teachers."* In A. Hargreaves (Ed.) *Rethinking Educational Change with Heart and Mind.* Alexandria, VA: Association for Supervision and Curriculum Development.

Marzano, R. Pickering, D.J., and Pollack, J.E. (2001). *Classroom Instruction that Works.* Alexandria, VA: Association for Supervision and Curriculum Development.

Marzano, R. (2003). *What Works: Translating Research into Action.* Alexandria, VA: Association for Supervision and Curriculum Development.

Ortega, M. (2005). *Presentation to Thompson School District Administrators.* Loveland, CO.

Paul, R. and Elder, L. (2002). *Critical Thinking: Tools for Taking Charge of Your Professional and Personal Life.* Upper Saddle River, NJ: Prentice Hall.

Piaget, J. (1977). *The Development of Thought: Equilibration of Cognitive Structures.* (A. Rosin, Trans.) New York: Viking Press.

Quinn, R. (1996). *Deep Change.* San Francisco: Jossey-Bass.

Quinn, R. (2004). *Building the Bridge As You Walk On It: A Guide for Leading Change.* San Francisco: Jossey-Bass.

Webster's Ninth Collegiate Dictionary. (1991). Springfield, MA: Merriam-Webster.